STOP SMOKING MADE E-Z

Provided by the Tobacco Control Resource Program, Office of Public Health, County of San Diego, with Proposition 99 funds under Grant No.: 89-97926 with the California Department of Health Services, Tobacco Control Section.

Materials distributed by the Serra Cooperative Library System

Gerald (JJ) Esopenko

MADE E-Z PRODUCTS, Inc.
Deerfield Beach, Florida / www.MadeE-Z.com

Stop Smoking Made E-Z™
© 2000 Made E-Z Products, Inc.
Printed in the United States of America

384 South Military Trail
Deerfield Beach, FL 33442
Tel. 954-480-8933
Fax 954-480-8906

http://www.MadeE-Z.com

1 2 3 4 5 6 7 8 9 10   CPC   R   10 9 8 7 6 5 4 3 2

This publication is designed to provide accurate and authoritative information in regard to subject matter covered. It is sold with the understanding that neither the publisher nor author is engaged in rendering legal, accounting, or other professional services. If legal advice or other expert assistance is required, the services of a competent professional should be sought. From: *A Declaration of Principles jointly adopted by a Committee of the American Bar Association and a Committee of Publishers.*

Stop Smoking Made E-Z™
Gerald (JJ) Esopenko

Table of contents

Introduction to Stop Smoking Made E-Z™

JJ's Jagged Journey

At 38-years-old my life was a mess. I was broke in every sense of the word. My wife and two small kids were on welfare while I was drowning in a sea of alcohol, despair and self-pity. I just didn't know what to do. Somehow, crime seemed to be the answer.

But, crime was not the answer. I came to, in a prison hospital. The first thing I saw was an angry-looking armed cop staring at me. I looked down and discovered I was handcuffed to the bed—shackled! Suddenly the horrible reality sunk in. "I'm in jail. I've been shot! What have I done?"

The pain covered me like a fog. I was dying for a drink. But through all this physical and mental anguish, do you know what I needed more than anything? I needed a cigarette. I swear I would have cut a finger off for a cigarette.

Well, with some time behind bars and the help of Alcoholics Anonymous, I never drank again, but I smoked for another dozen years.

I sure have had my share of problems. For the longest time, I couldn't resist junk food. If it wasn't made of sugar or fat, I wasn't interested. And gambling! If it moved, I had to bet on it. Gambling became a pit of quicksand; the more I struggled, the deeper I sank. But, this problem was cured pretty much instantly when I had to face my wife and tell her we had to get a $17,000 loan to pay off my bookmakers. One of life's precious moments.

From the "School of Hard Knocks", it was on to the "University of Adversity."

Later came a five-year affair with an alluring, magnetic lady. Her name was cocaine. She led me to a wondrous place, a place where there was no pain, no cares, no worries, no responsibilities. A place where everything seemed possible. But like my old friend, the cigarette, she had another side— a dark side. She demanded more time, more money, more attention. She wouldn't leave me alone. She wouldn't give me any peace. The final breakup was *absolute hell*. But I know now if I hadn't done it, this lady would have walked me to my grave.

In their time, each of these compulsions seemed as important as life itself. But I beat all of them on the first or second try, except (you guessed it) cigarettes, those *tenacious cigarettes!* It was Mark Twain who said, "Why, quitting cigarettes is easy. I've done it a thousand times." Well, I've done it plenty of times, usually only for a few hours, but twice for over a year. But, I never had a plan. For whatever reason, I would get disgusted, throw the pack away, make a vow and put my willpower to work.

Every hour and every day without a cigarette was slow torture. Temptation lurked around every corner. I was a shell of a man, alone, isolated. Every smoker became my idol. Life was dull and boring and useless. *Life was empty!* I felt so sorry for myself. I just never expected to be really happy again.

And fear! Fear surrounded me like a pack of hyenas, waiting to attack. I was scared of falling apart. I had a constant fear of failure, but even worse, a fear of success. Because success would mean, *forever,* a world without cigarettes.

So it was only a question of time until I weakened, sneaked that first delicious cigarette, then another, and within days I was back to being their full-time slave. Feeling defeated and humiliated, but at the same time, elated! My friends were back. *Life had meaning again!*

I admire people who can quit with willpower alone. Now that takes guts. It takes guts to stand that torment, usually for months, often for years, sometimes for life.

I found a solution, one that didn't push the human spirit to the breaking point. This is how I did it. I analyzed all my past experience, the failures as well as the successes, my time with Alcoholics Anonymous and Narcotics Anonymous. I studied all sorts of smoking cessation methods, plans and theories, books on addictions and compulsions. I really got into this thing! And I learned why we do what we do, what makes us function, from the leaders in the field of human behavior: people like Napoleon Hill, Brian Tracy, Susan Jeffers and Tony Robbins.

Finally, it all made sense. I drew up a plan, worked the plan and within a few weeks it was over, it was done, it was finished—and I was free. And, you know what? For the first time *I was happy! I truly didn't want to smoke anymore.* It was as close to a miracle as I ever expect to get. After smoking two to three packs a day for well over 30 years, there I was, with only a few fleeting wisps of urges and cravings, honestly and sincerely able to proclaim myself *a happy ex-smoker.*

It was two and a half years later that I ran across a survey in which 99% of smokers, given the chance again, would never start, and 94% wanted to quit. It suddenly struck me that this step system I had devised, this plan that had worked so amazingly well for me, could work as well for anyone. I would love smokers to find what I have found, to feel what I feel.

It sure can be hard to make the decision to quit. I should know. I spent years creating alibis and excuses that eventually took on the look of truth. Here are some of my favorites:

- Cigarettes are my only vice. No one should be perfect.
- I've been good in so many ways. Cigarettes are my reward.
- They can't be as bad as they say or they'd be illegal.
- I could get hit by a truck tomorrow.
- Fate determines when you die. When your number is up, your number is up.
- I'm only smoking low-tar cigarettes.

- My neighbor had a friend whose cousin's grandfather smoked like a chimney till he was 94.
- I need them to relax. There's so much stress in my life.
- I really truly enjoy smoking.
- You have to be ready to quit. I'm just not ready.

And the best one,

- Everyone deserves a little pleasure in life.

I worked at believing all this. I wanted to believe this. Then I heard a line that changed me forever: "It's the losers of the world that can't make a decision to save themselves." This struck me where it hurt. Deep down, I knew I had been fooling myself. Deep down, I was guilty and ashamed to be a smoker. My time had come.

A guide to the game

Chapter 1
A guide to the game

What you'll find in this chapter:

- ➠ The motivation to quit
- ➠ What to know about smoking's effects
- ➠ The key to quitting successfully
- ➠ Developing a desire to quit
- ➠ The steps of a quitting program

It's a rare person who wants to hear what he doesn't want to hear.

—Dick Cavett

Honest criticism is hard to take, particularly from a relative, a friend, an acquaintance or a stranger.

—Franklin P. Jones

Your time has come. Within a month, you won't be smoking, you won't *want* to smoke and you'll never smoke again. Sound too good to be true? Well, I'm not here to deceive or trick you. You deserve no less than the truth. We're entering into a partnership and the basis of all good partnerships is honesty. If you fail, I fail. I've worked long and hard to ensure that we succeed. I have done all the study, the legwork, the endless hours over a hot computer, the trials and errors. The hard part is over, and you get to share in the discovery of a system of thoughts and actions that will forever improve every facet of your life. We're going to be winners! Believe it or not, you will soon see, *This isn't a problem; it's an opportunity*. While exorcising cigarettes from your body, you will learn a formula that will help you more easily get all the good things in life.

> *Opportunity is missed by most people because it often comes dressed in overalls and looks like work.*
>
> —Thomas Edison

Commitment to change

 Partner, let's get to it! In one quick month it will be over, once and for all. First, I need your pledge to make these changes and commitments:

1) For three to four weeks you'll have to free up a total of 1 to 1-1/2 hours per day. This is a busy, fast-paced world and it won't always be easy to find the needed minutes. But I'm hoping that in the next few days you begin to realize that this brief partnership is more important than anything or anyone else, at this particular time, that demands your time or energy. Make my #1 priority *your* #1 priority.

2) You have to keep an open mind, be willing to question and challenge and change your attitudes, beliefs and opinions. Understand that smoking has the power to cloud and distort your thinking. A cigarette is the ultimate "con man." It bamboozles, swindles, dupes, outwits and hoodwinks; and the sucker is always the last to know. Accept that what you think and believe might be biased or perhaps even wrong. Be less rigid, more flexible.

> *If you think the way you have always thought, and do what you have always done, you will get the results you have always gotten.*
>
> —James Mapes

If need be, just pretend that everything I state is true and right. Occasionally in life you have to put your trust in a person you don't really know. I hope this is one of those times. Stick with me and, together, we'll ship this "con" back to the boondocks.

    3) Regardless of how you feel about various exercises—that they may be of little value, or perhaps trivial—just plain decide to do them. They are pieces in a jigsaw puzzle. The parts may not make sense until all are fitted into the big picture.

It's possible you're going through a patch of doubt and uncertainty right about now, but stay close to me and I'll show you the way. This is going to be a trip you will never forget. We're on our way to a wonderful place, a place you'll cherish in the years to come.

The real secret of success is enthusiasm.
—Walter Chrysler

The willingness to do creates the ability to do.
—Peter McWilliams

The facts about smoking

Before we go any further here are a few things you should know:

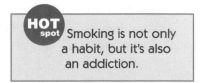
HOT spot Smoking is not only a habit, but it's also an addiction.

There is an obsessive or compulsive need to surrender. Smoking is not an option. The nicotine in inhaled smoke reaches the brain in 7 seconds. There it jump starts the nervous system, increasing alertness, easing pain and unleashing brain chemicals that cause ripples of pleasure. Nicotine targets the same "pleasure center" as cocaine and amphetamines. A one pack a day smoker repeats this assault 100,000 times a year.

Continued smoking actually changes the brain. Smokers develop far more of the proteins and receptors that respond to nicotine. A "need" has been established, one that is aggressively demanding. They need it just to feel *normal*. If nicotine is not received "on time," withdrawal sets in; anxiety, then anger, uneasiness and nervousness. You are rewarded for lighting up, and punished when you can't or don't. As one woman smoker put it, "It's like being in love with a man who's no good. You know you're a fool but you just can't help it."

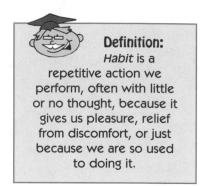

Definition:
Habit is a repetitive action we perform, often with little or no thought, because it gives us pleasure, relief from discomfort, or just because we are so used to doing it.

Your brain is designed to work best with familiar and established habit patterns, (comfort zones). For example, think about your morning routine: using the toilet, brushing your teeth, showering, drying, shaving or applying make-up, and so on. You can likely complete this procedure with a bare minimum of thought. Why is this? Because you have performed these needs over and over again, your subconscious has learned (memorized) each as a mental habit pattern, *something you want or need,* and automatically gives you the thoughts and actions required to carry out all the functions. All these habit patterns are combined into a operating program where the movements and order remain pretty much the same every day. Somewhat like a computer, your morning routine is "programmed" in your brain. The subconscious is wired to help give you what you want, to save time, effort and energy.

note

You have been "programmed" to smoke. Without you being much aware, a dozen or two mental habit patterns have been established in your brain, and woven together into a dominant behavior program. One is so strong that it has become a compulsion. But this program, *your desire and craving to smoke,* is protected by a combination lock, one to which we have the numbers. Once inside, we are free to make changes, to "reprogram."

We first make our habits, then our habits make us.

—John Dryden

Making the choice to change

When confronted with any new behavior or thought process, your subconscious gives you feelings of discomfort or anxiety. Do you remember playing the guitar or piano for the first time, or golfing or skiing, or learning algebra or a new language? It was awkward and confusing and frustrating. These were activities outside of your *comfort zones*. Your brain didn't know how to react, what to do. But if you persisted past the discomfort, a new pattern was born, growing in strength and size. The skill level followed accordingly. You studied and practiced the guitar, and suddenly you were making actual, coherent music.

Realize that when you first start working with the ideas in this book, you may feel uncomfortable. Your brain is resisting the unfamiliar, wanting to remain in the same place. Inertia. It's like pushing a car—difficult to get it moving, but once it starts rolling, it takes less and less effort.

You should welcome this discomfort because getting out of your comfort zones is where all the fun is. This is where you learn, discover, become more capable. This is where your world expands with new levels of happiness and achievement and self-esteem. Believe me, this is where you want to be.

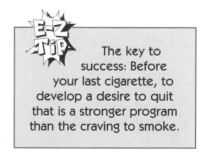

The key to success: Before your last cigarette, to develop a desire to quit that is a stronger program than the craving to smoke.

Just think about it. When you happily quit smoking, think how strong, dynamic, how competent you'll feel. You're going to be so proud of yourself. And it's only a few weeks away!

You can choose to continue to smoke right up to your *Quit Day.* You'll pick the date during Step 3, likely to be around two weeks from now. Our goal during this interim

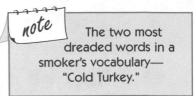

note The two most dreaded words in a smoker's vocabulary— "Cold Turkey."

period is to dismantle and disable the "smoking program" (like continually scratching a phonograph record) and in its place build a new comfort zone, one in which the dominant desire is to **not** smoke.

Think how remarkable it will be to actually be ready, willing and able, on the day you have chosen, to leave cigarettes in the dust.

In my estimate, the addiction of smoking is less than 20% physical and more than 80% mental. This is why the vast majority who attempt to quit, with willpower or nicotine replacement aids alone fail. They simply do not deal adequately with the mental aspect.

Cold Turkey and nicotine replacement

Let's look at this in a little more detail. A popular quitting method is Cold Turkey (simply abstaining from smoking but with no real plan or strategy). This is the way I see it: if Cold Turkey takes 90% willpower, the failure rate is around 90%. Nicotine replacement helps with the physical aspect but still requires 80% willpower, with the resulting failure rate over 80%.

And keep in mind that those who do manage to quit using either of these two methods experience painful urges and cravings, often far into the future. At best, I would classify this group as marginally successful ex-smokers. Those that are fully successful suffer a bare minimum of pain, for a minimum period of time.

Our goal is to tackle the mental side of tobacco addiction, to get your head and your thinking turned around so that, when the day for your last cigarette arrives, only a fraction of willpower is needed. Minimal willpower equals minimal pain.

A day or two before your quit day, you will be in a better position to decide whether you want to use Zyban, Nicoderm, Habitrol or Nicorette. I certainly have no objection. If you feel it may help, go right ahead.

Many people feel they are controlled by some strange, mysterious force that dooms them to a life-time of failure and frustration. Nothing could be farther from the truth. We make our own luck, good and bad.

> *Success is simply a matter of luck. Ask any failure.*
> —Earl Wilson

Flying free

Somewhere along the way, I realized that everything I would become was up to me. No one was going to do it for me. Until then I had the conscious expectation that somewhere, somehow, someone was still responsible for me and my situation. Not so. Whether my parents had or had not raised me to be a totally self-reliant individual was of no relevance. I was in charge of my destiny. I was in the driver's seat.

> *note* The acceptance of personal responsibility was not easy; it was one of the hardest things I have ever done.

I used to operate on excuses, blaming my problems on bad timing, bad luck, on other people, or random circumstances, always looking for reasons why something couldn't be done. When I was suddenly forced to give up my excuses, it was like the first time I jumped out of a plane. Never was I as alone and vulnerable as at the moment I let go of that strut. But then, a rush of excitement, and I was flying free.

This reminds me of a "fatherhood" story. On his 12th birthday, my son Jay's wish was to parachute. However, after making a phone call, I gave him the "bad news," "Sorry, kid, you have to be 16." He was disappointed, but made me promise to take him up in four years. Sure, no problem. "And how about you, Dad, will you jump with me?" Few things terrified me more, but I felt I had to say "yes," to appear to be the brave man he thought I was. After all, once he discovered girls, this would likely be forgotten.

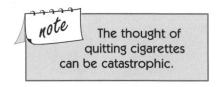

note The thought of quitting cigarettes can be catastrophic.

Well, it was forgotten, but by me, not him. After a woeful hour of "instruction," there we were, with a pilot and a jump master, very slowly shaking and crawling to 3,000 feet, in a dilapidated Cessna that I'd wager had to be 40 years old. "What in the hell was I doing here? What was I thinking?"

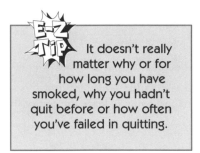

E-Z TIP It doesn't really matter why or for how long you have smoked, why you hadn't quit before or how often you've failed in quitting.

The jump master opened the door and suddenly we were in a mini tornado. Not being able to be heard above the roar, he gestured to me. The moment of truth had arrived. Through the howling wind I desperately tried to remember the routine; left foot on step, right hand on wing strut, left hand on strut, spread-eagle and let go. But then I froze. "Release!" he was screaming, "Release!" I couldn't let go. Catastrophe was waiting. Either I'd drop like a stone, or be cut in half by the tail wing. Then I glanced left, saw my son's hopeful face, clenched my teeth and decided to die like a man. Seconds later the chute popped open and I was lazily floating to earth, more alive than I could ever remember.

The first and best victory is to conquer self. To be conquered by self is, of all things, the most shameful and vile.

—Plato

At this moment, you may be going through some negative emotions, apprehension, dread, insecurity, a little sinking sensation in your stomach and some degree of fear. If you are, just understand that this is a natural reaction to having your comfort zone threatened by something new. This won't last long. The more you get into this book, the better you'll feel. Wait and see. In the meantime, relax and go with the flow.

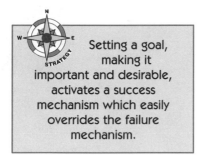

Setting a goal, making it important and desirable, activates a success mechanism which easily overrides the failure mechanism.

Realize that the past is over, important only for what you have learned. Leave behind all apologies, regrets and disappointments. Don't waste any energy on what has come and gone. What is important is today, tomorrow and the future.

The past does not equal the future.

—Tony Robbins

DEFINITION

Denial can take the form of failing to see what is, or seeing it and resisting, because you don't like it. Let others live in a fog of self-deception. Take off the blinders, deal with the truth and you will leave the rest of the herd in the dust.

There is a natural tendency, some call it a *failure* mechanism, to follow the path of least resistance, to move towards immediate gratification with little or no concern for the long-term consequences. Most people allow their desire for what is fun, easy and convenient to determine most of what they do.

Don't be overly concerned about having to understand every concept or idea in this book. You don't have to know how electricity works to turn on the lights. Just learn where the switches are located.

Making the most of this guide

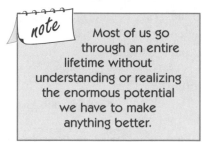

I suggest you carry this book along with you every waking hour. Take every opportunity available to fill your mind with "good" thoughts and ideas. The more you read and absorb, the quicker and easier the process.

There's a personal journal at the end of the book where you might want to record your daily progress.

> *It is a major indictment against the world's educational system, that most people come into this world, live their span of years, and pass on without being aware of their mind power, and the fact that their lives are made or unmade by this mind power.*
>
> —Napoleon Hill

note

Most of us go through an entire lifetime without understanding or realizing the enormous potential we have to make anything better.

The greatest of all assets in this world is the human brain. But, of all assets, it the least utilized and most abused. Experts tell us we use far less than 10% of its capacity. That leaves over 90% in untapped mental powers. At birth we're not given an owner's manual. (As a comparison, imagine, having never used one before, you buy a computer, set it up in your home but find there are no operating instructions.) In Step 1 we explore a fascinating subject, the workings of the brain.

All success begins with desire. Step 2 reveals smoking facts, myths and lies that may shock you into reality. You'll never look at a cigarette the same way again. If you squirm and sweat, good! Discomfort is the kindling for the fires of change. Your beliefs guide your behavior. To change what you do, we have to change what you believe. This is the basis of Step 3.

Step 4 is where you take charge, decide enough is enough, where you get mad. You make a committed decision and set your Quit Day. It sounds scary but it's likely you'll feel a surge of confidence and a cathartic sense of relief.

Attitude is everything. When you feel good, you get things done. This is the focus of the next step. Positive thinking is where you'll find some of the switches that light the rooms of your mind.

Smoking becomes a behavioral "super highway." The appeal of the "open road" is overwhelming. In Step 6 we use every device and obstacle available to make this road "undrivable."

By the time you get to your quit day, Step 7, you have a whole new perspective on our "friend," the cigarette. The urge to smoke has lost much of its importance and allure, while the desire to quit has grown wings. Your weapons and tactics are in place for the final brief withdrawal battle with the addiction demon. Victory and freedom are just over the next hill.

Brain power

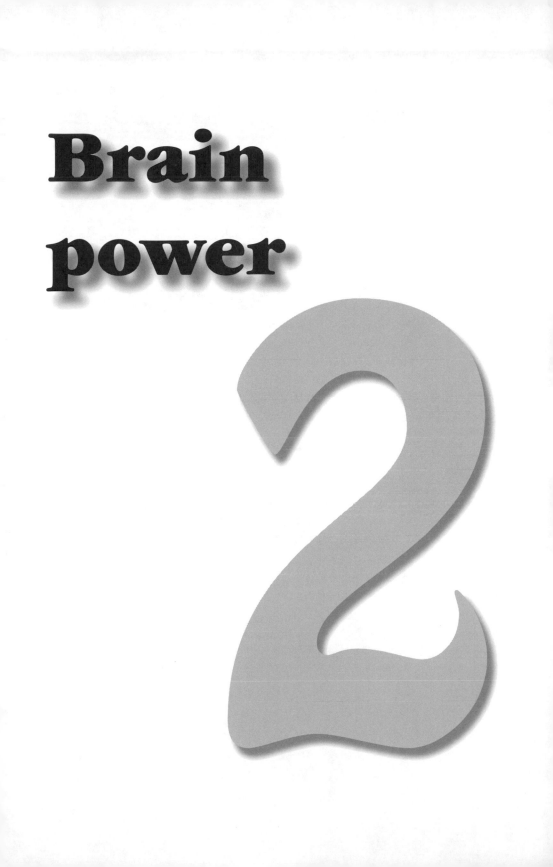

Chapter 2

Brain power

Deep within man dwell those slumbering powers; powers that would astonish, that he never dreamed of possessing; forces that would revolutionize his life if aroused and put into action.

—Orison Swett Marden

Men ought to know that from nothing else but the brain come joys, delights, laughter, sorrows, grieves, despondency and lamentations.

—Hippocrates 400 B.C.

The human brain is the most complex structure in the universe. It defies even the most advanced computer technology. Each of its 28 billion neurons acts like a tiny computer and together they can process 30 billion bits of information per second. The fastest computer can make connections only one at a time, **but** a reaction in a neuron can spread to hundreds of thousands of others in one-tenth the time it takes to blink your eye.

How the brain functions

We have two ways of processing information:

1) Operating during our waking hours, the conscious mind makes decisions, exercises willpower, gives commands to the subconscious, decides and determines what is right or wrong, good or bad, true or untrue.

2) The subconscious mind is somewhat like a computer in that it does not think. It is simply a gigantic memory bank, a storehouse or file cabinet that holds all your experiences, everything that has ever happened to you, everything that has entered your conscious mind. By the age of 21, you have already stored more than 100 times the contents of the entire Encyclopedia Britannica.

note The subconscious cannot judge right from wrong, bad from good, true from untrue.

The job of the subconscious mind is to accumulate and retrieve data and to respond exactly the way you are programmed or the way you have programmed yourself. It holds your memories, attitudes, emotions, beliefs and habits. It knows all your comfort zones and works to keep you in them.

Anything accepted by the conscious mind is filed away to be used in making future decisions. Once a pattern is noticed, the subconscious will give us the actions, thoughts, feelings and behavior that fit that pattern. In essence, it gives us what it perceives we want. Our brains are instinctually wired to help keep us away from pain and into pleasure. (This may or may not be actual pain and pleasure, but

HOT spot One very significant fact: Our emotions have far more effect on what we say and do, than logic or reason.

how *we see or perceive* pain and pleasure. A masochist loves being whipped.)

There is no sense of time in the subconscious: thoughts of the past, present and future are all registered alike. Negative thoughts and actions are treated the same as positive input. It can't differentiate between a real or imagined experience. *Feelings guide us to a much greater degree than intellect.*

 note Whenever there's a conflict between the two minds, the subconscious usually wins.

Here's an example: You're walking along the beach on a very hot, sunny day. Your mouth is parched and your body is baking. Coming towards you is an ice cream vendor. You have only seconds to make a decision. Your conscious mind says, "Stay away from that sugar and animal fat. It will clog your arteries, rot your teeth and make you fat." A rational, logical argument. You hesitate. Then the subconscious is heard from, "You've been so good, you deserve a treat. Anyway, you're starting a diet next week. It's only one cone, not the end of the world. It's so hot! It would taste so-o-o good."

HOT spot Which way do you think the decision would go? Yes, most of us would succumb to the temptation. Feelings score more points than reason.

The brain's pathways

Each time you learn something or find a new meaning or association, your brain center creates new memory pathways by organizing the way the cells connect to each other. Repeated signals tend to take the same pathway every time. These pathways

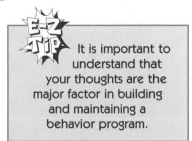 **E-Z TIP** It is important to understand that your thoughts are the major factor in building and maintaining a behavior program.

are made between neurons by way of tiny links called synapses. Repetition develops more synapses and the response becomes automatic (remember the example of the guitar or learning a new language). A behavior like smoking is so pervasive, intense and repetitious that the pathway becomes a super highway (a dominant program). You are compelled to follow that route over and over again.

Each thought activates electrical energy that links neurons with synapses. The stronger and deeper you feel about something, the greater the effect on the program. Emotion is the fuel that powers your thoughts.

We are what we think. All that we are arises with our thoughts. With our thoughts we make our world.

—Buddha

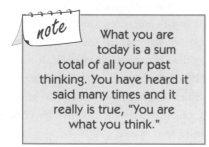

note What you are today is a sum total of all your past thinking. You have heard it said many times and it really is true, "You are what you think."

One simple example of how a pathway is formed is learning a new telephone number. If you want it stored in the subconscious, you might close your eyes, concentrate hard and repeat that number over and over. Each time you do, more neurons are linked by synapses in the same pattern until the number is "learned," until a pathway has been developed into a mental-habit pattern. Later, when you need that number, you can recall it by a command from your conscious mind to the subconscious; in effect, "What is my phone number?" The more it's used, the stronger the pattern. If it is not used, the pattern connections break down. This is why I can still remember the home phone number that I used for 20 years, thirty years ago—but forgot a number I had for a year, just five years ago.

Every man is what he is because of the dominating thoughts which he permits to occupy his mind. Thoughts which a man deliberately places in his own mind and encourages with sympathy, and which he mixes with one or more of the emotions, constitute the motivating forces which direct and control his every movement, act and deed.

—Napoleon Hill

The brain is continually being changed, remodeled and rebuilt. It analyzes incoming information, compares it with past experience and forges new connections, new pathways. Synapses appear and disappear. When an established pattern is used less and less it becomes transformed, weakens and in a fairly short period of time, will all but disappear.

Your subconscious is enormously powerful. But one must be careful; it can be used for creation or destruction, good or evil. It works, unquestioningly, day and night to make your behaviors fit a pattern consistent with your emotionalized hopes, thoughts and desires. Most people let their minds roam free, allowing chance and accident to determine its direction and destination. If you permit your inner mind to work on its own, to program itself, you are simply asking for trouble. If your subconscious mind is a garden, the conscious mind is the gardener. If care and planning are used in the planting and the tending, flowers flourish with color and vitality. Left on its own, weeds will choke all the good and the worthwhile and the beautiful.

> *The subconscious is the best of servants but the worst of masters.*
>
> —Nathaniel Emmons

Programming

Your "smoking" program has been memorized over some period of time. Memory is learning. There can be no learning without memory. We memorize in three ways:

1) Impression

DEFINITION

Impressions are received in the conscious mind by our five senses: sight, smell, sound, touch and taste, and are registered in the subconscious. (Remember, your subconscious can't distinguish between the real and the imagined—if you can deeply and vividly imagine biting into a bitter lemon, your inner mind will record and utilize the information the same as the actual action itself). Five minutes of concentrated, energetic thinking can produce more powerful and lasting impressions on your mind than days of vague, unorganized thought.

Above all, we are visually minded. The nerves that lead from the eye to the brain are 25 times as large as those from the ear. We think best in pictures. Often we forget a man's name in minutes, but remember his face for years.

At times, one impression will last a lifetime. Do you remember the time you touched a hot stove? Probably. When intense pain is registered, a massive number of neurons are linked together, forming an instant pathway, an immediate habit pattern. It's likely you learned a lesson that was never forgotten.

Emotional pain, like some horrible embarrassment, can have a similar long-term impact. It was over 40 years ago, but I'll never forget standing in front of a laughing class, stuttering, unable to get the words out. Beet red, wanting desperately to cry, or to die.

Intense pleasure also leaves a strong impression. I thought my first line of cocaine was a gift from the heavens. For a half hour I was no longer a failure or a loser, depressed or angry. Suddenly I was bursting with confidence and optimism. I was somebody. Can you see how easy it is to become an addict? To be able to go from a position of pain to instant pleasure? Can you see more clearly how the mind works? Your conscious mind may know about the dangers of a particular drug. Logic and reason might prevail but it's up against a powerful force. The subconscious is wired to keep you out of pain and into pleasure, and what better way to achieve both than a hit of cocaine, or heroin, or nicotine. The subconscious does not have the capability to judge good from bad, right from wrong.

2)   Association

Your mind is an associating machine. It constantly links related information and data together to form or fit patterns. Consider the various associations made with smoking: coffee breaks, post sex, alcohol, relaxation,and perhaps dozens more. Coffee without a smoke can be more of an ordeal than a pleasure. If the cigarette is not there after sex, panic sets in. Relax? Without a cigarette?

3) *Repetition*

By far, the most important factor in memorization and learning is repetition. Repeating a thought or action links more neurons together to strengthen a program pathway. At some point the behavior becomes conditioned, pretty much automatic.

It's plain to see why smoking is such a powerful program. Every day hundreds of thoughts and actions related to some aspect of smoking are generated and filed. How many times a day do you think about a cigarette, light up, fill your lungs, flick an ash, smoke while working, or playing, or concentrating, or relaxing, or watching TV, or driving? Smoking becomes an integral part of your daily routine.Over and over and over and over again.

We are what we repeatedly do.

—Aristotle

To reiterate, your subconscious is designed to help keep you away from pain and into pleasure, and determines which is which, by your desires,your habit patterns, whatever you do over and over. The combination of these patterns form a behavior program, a comfort zone. The subconscious has an easy route (program) to follow. It gives you thoughts and actions that fit the behavior program, that keep you in your comfort zone, away from pain and in pleasure.

Challenging the comfort zone

Any attempt to change or challenge this comfort zone will, at least initially, cause you to feel physically and/or emotionally uncomfortable or anxious. Part of Step 1 is understanding and accepting that you will, for a while, feel awkward, and uncomfortable. But these feelings won't last long.

> ⚠️ **CAUTION** Even thinking about doing something different from what you're accustomed to will make you feel tense and uneasy.

Scales of desire

Imagine a set of scales where the right side indicates your *desire to quit,* to not smoke, and the left side your *craving to smoke,* the desire to smoke. The balance is determined by the strength and quantity (the weight) of all the mental habit patterns that make up each operating program. Let's look at the factors that make up the "weight" on each side:

1) Craving to smoke program

This has been formed by the following mental habit patterns of thoughts and actions:

- your positive beliefs about smoking

- physical cravings (addiction)

- associations with coffee, alcohol, work, play, TV, driving, etc.

- pain of withdrawal

- relaxation (perceived)

- advertising

- self-concept (how you see yourself)

- conditioning (repetition of thoughts and actions)

- any favorable thought towards smoking triggers (something that ignites an urge to smoke—perhaps you always smoke when talking on the phone, or when in your car)

- various pleasures

2) Desire to quit (to not smoke) program

This was formed by the following mental habit patterns of thoughts and actions:

- health threat

- coughing

- terrible taste late in day

- social pressure

- cost in dollars

- loss of control in one's life

- inconvenience

- feeling of weakness, of slavery

- self-loathing

- fear of early death

- negative role model

- self-esteem

- cleanliness

- any unfavorable thought towards smoking

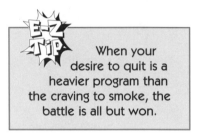

Both lists are incomplete, but at first glance they appear to be somewhat equal or competitive. You have both programs in your brain, but as a smoker you know that the craving to smoke is much stronger than the desire to quit. One program is totally dominant over the second. The *craving to smoke* tray on the scales is very heavy while the *desire to quit* tray is light. The smoking program is strong and established. You are compelled to continue to smoke. Your subconscious is driven by the stronger, heavier (dominant) program to give you the thoughts, actions and feelings to keep you into pleasure (smoking) and away from the pain of not smoking (withdrawal, sense of loss, threat to comfort zone, etc.).

> **E-Z TIP**
>
> When your desire to quit is a heavier program than the craving to smoke, the battle is all but won.

So, in order to make a change, the obvious strategy is to lower the "weight" on the left side, that is, to lower the craving for cigarettes, and to add "weight" to the right side, increase the desire to quit. How do we do this? Let's first look at the *craving side*. All the actions (patterns) either provide pleasure (relaxation, stimulation, association with a drink or a cup or coffee, the anticipation of a cigarette) or a way to avoid pain (the anxiety of withdrawal, the feelings of emptiness or loneliness, of something missing). What we do is direct and focus thinking to turn everything around as much as possible, to reduce the pleasure and add lots of pain. On the *desire side,* we do the opposite, add pleasure and reduce pain. Any "weight" added to the right side automatically lightens the left and vice versa. Our goal is to "tip the scales" by your quit day.

Natural laws of human behavior

Brian Tracy, a noted expert on human behavior, formulated a number of natural laws which help us to understand and guide our minds. These are laws because they are exact, dependable, predictable and timeless.

- The **Law of Concentration**—says that whatever you dwell upon grows. The more you think about something the more it becomes part of your reality. Whatever you think about on a continual basis becomes a part of yourself. You become what you think about.

- The **Law of Substitution**—states that your conscious mind can only hold one thought at a time. At any time, you can substitute a negative or destructive thought for one that is beneficial and positive. You can always choose to think about something helpful, rather than harmful. If you keep your mind focused on where you want to go and what you want to accomplish, this becomes your reality. Focus on the future rather than the past. Spend 5% of your time on the problem and 95% on the solution.

- The **Law of Expectations**—whatever we expect with confidence becomes our own self-fulfilling prophecy. We continually act as our own fortune tellers by the way we talk to ourselves about how we expect things to turn out. We tend to fulfill the expectations we have of ourselves, whether it be high or low, positive or negative. Expect the best and you'll get the best.

> **HOT** spot Whatever you believe with feeling becomes your reality.

Successful people expect to be successful, to be happy and they are seldom disappointed. Unsuccessful people have an attitude of negative expectation, of cynicism and pessimism, that causes situations to work out exactly as they expect as well.Imagine if you walked around all day expecting good things to happen, expecting everything to work out for your benefit. Think about how much more optimistic and cheerful you would be.

- The **Law of Subconscious Activity**—any idea or thought that you accept as true in your conscious mind will be accepted without question by your subconscious mind. And your subconscious will immediately begin working to bring it into your reality, making all your words, feelings, actions and body language fit a pattern consistent with your dominant thoughts.

- The **Law of Attraction**—each human is a living magnet. You radiate thought energy and invariably attract into your life the people and circumstances that harmonize with your dominant thoughts.

- The **Law of Belief**—your beliefs form a screen of logic or prejudice through which you see the world and you attempt to never allow any information that doesn't fit. Even though certain beliefs are completely erroneous, to the degree to which you believe them to be true, they are true for you. Beliefs can originate in childhood, from movies or books or hearsay, and can be based on entirely false information.

- The **Law of Control**—says that you feel positive about yourself to the degree to which you feel you are in control of your own life. You feel negative about yourself to the degree to which you feel you are not in control, or that you're being controlled by some external force or person or influence. Too often passengers end up in places they don't want to be. You want the steering wheel of life in your hands.

Well, I hope you're starting to get a feel for where all this is going. For now you may be a passenger, but the controls will soon be in your hands. And it may be a trip quite different from the one you expected.

What are the 5 things you most value in your life?

What are the five most important components of your life? What would you sacrifice for, pay the most for, stand up for, fight for? Prepare and complete your own list before you proceed to the next chapter.

Truth and conse-
quences

3

Chapter 3
Truth and consequences

Men stumble over the truth from time to time, but most pick themselves up and hurry off as if nothing happened.

—Winston Churchill

The white man and the red man came face to face at a crucial juncture in history, and the first thing they did was exchange vices. Columbus introduced the Indians to alcohol and in no time alcoholism spread across North America like wildfire. He found the natives smoking tobacco, mostly in connection with religious rituals, brought it back home with him, and within two generations virtually the entire male population of Western Europe was hooked on smoking tobacco.

—Dr. Ralph Cinque

The cigarette profile

Picture the first drag of the first cigarette of your day. Satisfying? Absolutely. Tasty? Perhaps. Relaxing? Definitely. But that lung full of smoke contains 4,000 chemicals and compounds (many of them noxious, toxic, and over 40 that are carcinogenic—proven to cause cancer). They invade every inch of your body and brain within seconds, and begin a cycle that is repeated hundreds of times every single day. Cyanide, formaldehyde, ammonia, acetone, shellac, turpentine, nitrous oxide, polonium 210, and carbon monoxide continually course through your life-giving bloodstream. And, let's not forget nicotine—one drop can kill a cat.

How about the stuff we don't know about? Among the most tightly held secrets in the world are those formulas for flavorants, preservatives and texturizers concocted in the tobacco industry laboratories. You can bet the last thing they're concerned about is your health and well-being.

Here's one "flavorant" recipe that leaked out to the public: 2,6,6-trimethyl-1-(3 ethoxy-1-butenyl-cyclohex-1-ene). What on earth could this be? Isn't there an ad that beckons, "Come to where the flavor is, _____ country."

> *I don't care what they say, or what you believe, or what you learned in school, or what you thought it ought to be, I'm telling you how it is!*
>
> —Philip McGraw

The RJ Reynolds plant in Tobaccoville, North Carolina, churns out 110 billion (110,000,000,000) cigarettes per year with a work force of only 2,300.

With government and business constantly throwing billion dollar

> **HINT** Do you remember your first cigarette as a kid? Coughing, hacking, nausea, dizziness. Do you think our bodies were trying to tell us something?

figures around, we lose sight of the magnitude. Counting one number per second, 24 hours a day, reaching one billion would take 32 years! Stacking dollar bills, how high would a billion reach? 70 miles.

 A cigarette is such an ingenious way of delivering a drug. It's sleek and neat and attractive. You get to hold it, play with it, burn it, watch it. It's white and looks so innocent. And it's legal!

Advertising and promotion

How do they do it? How do they take this dirt-cheap weed that is filthy, smelly, dirty, dangerous and deadly and get so many of us to consume it on a regular basis? Well, they spare no expense in hiring those who best know the art of manipulating and controlling human behavior, the advertising agencies. And they think long term. We become targets at a very early age. They begin programming us early in life. Ads feature fresh, clean, pure, athletic, uncorrupted and attractive people. Promotions and sponsorships link our emotional good feelings about tennis, the arts, and car racing to cigarettes. Advertisers clearly understand what drives us is not intellect, but emotion. They are masters at influencing what we link to pleasure.

EZ TIP: Most smokers think they are totally unaffected by any ads or promotions, but from the time we are toddlers our subconscious minds are fed a steady diet of images linking cigarettes to purity, virility, peace, tranquillity, exciting lifestyles.

That special cadre of people who actively try to increase demand are low folk indeed. The marketers, ad executives, lobbyists and lawyers who fight for the right to fly tobacco banners up and down the beach have sold their souls.

—Andrew Tobias

Is it possible to get someone to do something destructive just by linking pleasure to it? You better believe it! These links or associations don't have to be true or right or logical or real. Our resistance weakens over the years. The fears and dangers seem overdone, irrational. How can we forego all that pleasure?

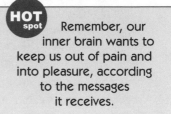

HOT spot Remember, our inner brain wants to keep us out of pain and into pleasure, according to the messages it receives.

Most smokers would sincerely deny being in any way swayed by tobacco advertising and promotion, but year after year, without our being aware of it, the programming continues. Finally, somewhere along the line, enough of us become convinced that with a cigarette we can be cool, daring, sophisticated, independent, strong, relaxed, sexy, popular, adventuresome. We get the acceptance and approval of our friends. We are breaking the rules, indulging in an "adult" amusement.

note To the cigarette manufacturers, every new smoker may be worth many tens of thousands of dollars in revenue.

Madison Avenue has done its job. A worthwhile percentage of kids have fallen into the trap. As always, the advertising dollars paid off handsomely.

More money is spent on advertising and promoting cigarettes in the United States than any other product. *Marlboro* is the largest selling packaged product on the globe.

Smoking is the world's #1 public health problem.

Cigarettes are simultaneously the source of more death and disability than any product ever invented, and also the object of the largest marketing effort ever devoted to any product.
—Kenneth Warner Ph.D.

I would be infinitely more comfortable representing John Gotti than the president of Phillip Morris. Their lawyers tend to talk about smoking in abstract terms like "liberty" and "rights," but all this is nonsense. Tobacco has no redeeming qualities. It is a killer, the most evil product on the face of the earth!

—Attorney Stanley Rosenblatt

The tobacco industry portrays smoking as an adult activity, an act of freedom, of choice. I get mad when I see they hooked me as a child. I was their puppet for 40 years. And I get mad when I picture these tobacco barons, in their luxurious boardrooms, counting their billions of dollars, our hard-earned dollars. And you know what? They see us as fools, as sheep. *They look down at us and laugh.*

When David Goerlitz, the model known as "the Winston Man" asked a tobacco company executive why he didn't smoke, the executive replied, "Are you kidding? We reserve that right for the young, the poor, the black, and the stupid."

Another responded "We don't smoke the crap, we just sell it."

Financial costs

It can seem to be a fairly insignificant amount, just a few dollars a day. "If I didn't buy cigarettes, I'd waste the money somewhere else." Is this wishful thinking or intentional deception?

Take a minute to roughly calculate what you spent on cigarettes thus far in your life. What will it cost you the next year? What other uses could you put this money to: an exciting vacation, a down payment on the car you always wanted, a new

> **HINT** Every year, by not smoking, you could have a chunk of cash available to play with. Every year for the rest of your life.

> *note* Smoking kills more people than AIDS, heroin, cocaine, alcohol, car accidents, fire, and murder combined. Smoking is responsible for one out of every five deaths in the United States.

stylish wardrobe, top of the line golf clubs, computer lessons and your own computer, a course to upgrade your education or skills?

If somehow I would have had the brains and the foresight to quit smoking at age 25, and invest the daily savings in a mutual fund, here are the results: at an average of $5 a day and a 10% return (mutual funds have generally performed much better than this), I would have $30,200 after 10 years. In 20 years the figure would have grown to $108,500. Today, 30 years later, here I could have sat, at age 55, counting $311,660. The magic of good sense, diligence and compound interest.

Men do not usually die, they kill themselves.
—Michael de Montaigne

The heart

Two-pack-a-day smokers suffer their first heart attacks at an average age of 51.

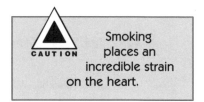

CAUTION Smoking places an incredible strain on the heart.

Here's what happens:

- Nicotine constricts the blood vessels and stimulates the heart, greatly increasing blood pressure and the work load.

- Mucus formed in the lungs impedes the exchange of oxygen and carbon dioxide.

- Carbon monoxide, a deadly poisonous gas produced by the burning of tobacco, robs the body of much of its oxygen. With the combination of CO and less oxygen to the brain, a smoker often suffers from lethargy, confusion and difficulty in thinking. (I know what you're thinking, "But smoking sharpens my concentration!" This is an illusion that I'll explain later.)

> **note** A smoker processes less oxygen at sea level than a non-smoker at 8,000 feet.

- Clotting agents in the blood become sticky, cluster, and play havoc with the entire cardio-vascular system.

- Bad cholesterol is manufactured, further clogging the arteries.

The heart. This small masterpiece of creation, the size of a grapefruit, the center of our being, works uncomplainingly every minute of every day of every year. But smokers crack the whip and demand more: They force their precious hearts to beat and pump, under the most difficult conditions, an extra 30,000 times a day.

Lung cancer

A one pack a day smoker deposits an 8 ounce cupful of carcinogen-rich, molasses-like tar into the lungs every year.

Picture this scene. For months you've had a persistent, unusual cough and a concerned someone convinces you to check it out. After a thorough examination the doctor shows you the X-ray, and with a somber look on his

HOT spot In the U.S. 250,000 women a year will die of heart attacks and another 250,000 of related coronary problems. A woman who has a heart attack is twice as likely as a man to die from it. If she doesn't die, she's twice as likely to have another attack.

face, says, "I'm very sorry. A tumor in your left lung is malignant. We'll need you in the hospital immediately."

After months of chemotherapy, radiation, surgery, you lie in bed utterly exhausted and defeated. Your hair is gone, your face and body are gaunt and wasted. You can't sleep. The pain has been terrible and endless.

The doctor walks in the room and his face tells the story. You suddenly realize all hope is gone. "I'm so sorry. We've tried everything, but the cancer has spread to your liver and brain. Nothing more can be done. I think it's time to make your final arrangements."

As you lie there, surrounded by the grim faces of your loved ones, thoughts flood your head. "How could I have been so stupid? What is there I can say to my family? There's so much I wanted to do. I'd give anything for just one more healthy year of life."

This is a scenario that's played out tens of thousands of times a year throughout North America. Most every victim is surprised and disbelieving when the diagnosis is delivered. They used to think, "It doesn't happen that often. It'll never happen to me." Now these words, "Oh God, why me?"

> *The doctors tell me that I have maybe five or six weeks to go because I have lung cancer caused by smoking. You face more danger with the 20 cigarettes that are in your pocket than any six bullets in somebody's gun. Cigarettes are a time bomb that you plant in your own life that explode 20 or 30 years later. The danger that threatened my life as a policeman was sitting in that radio car and lighting up that cigarette. I am 47 years old and I'll never see 48.*
>
> —Ken McFeeley
> New York City Policeman

I am haunted not only by the tobacco dead, but by the lungless, voiceless, bladderless, gullet-less, tongueless patients and those close to them who must also suffer.
We swim in a sea of carcinogens, in which the cigarette is the great white shark.

—William G. Cahan, M.D.
No Stranger To Tears

CAUTION

Just a few bare facts are needed, and it rarely gives early warning of its presence. Lung cancer is close to being a death sentence. The pain and suffering is truly something one can't rationally imagine. The reason more smokers don't get lung cancer is because heart disease kills them first. If the effects of cigarette smoking appeared on our skin rather than the lungs, no one would smoke. Enough said.

The human body is the best picture of the human soul.
—Ludwig Wittgenstein

Wayne McLaren, who portrayed the rugged *Marlboro Man* in cigarette ads died of lung cancer at 51 said "I'm dying proof that smoking will kill you."

Emphysema

DEFINITION

Emphysema is a disease that destroys the lung's elasticity and, therefore, its ability to inhale and exhale properly. Affected tissue can never be repaired or replaced and the

note Lung cancer kills more women than breast cancer.

disease progresses slowly but steadily. Patients spend years gasping for breath and, when death comes, it's usually from an overworked heart.

This is my most frightening smoking disease. For a period of time I had become addicted to nasal sprays and for months my breathing was difficult and exhausting. Four doctors mis-diagnosed the problem. The fifth prescribed a new medication, but I would have to stop using any spray. I was in a Las Vegas hotel room at 4 in the morning when I suffered a paralyzing panic attack. I was frozen in terror. I couldn't shake the dread that my breathing would never be normal again. But, thanks to this enlightened medical man, the new remedy worked and I was back to normal within a week. I will never forget that night.

I often think that someone should wheel my mother-in-law around to schools as an example of why not to smoke. Nobody was hipper or cooler than she was in her day. Now at age 62, she has emphysema; she can't walk and looks 82.

—Vicki T..

My name is Patrick Reynolds. My grandfather, R.J. Reynolds, founded the tobacco company that makes Camels, Winstons and Salems. My grandfather chewed tobacco and died of cancer. My father, R.J. Reynolds Jr., smoked heavily and died of emphysema. My mother smoked and had emphysema and heart disease. My two aunts, also smokers, died of emphysema and cancer. Currently, three of my older brothers who smoke have emphysema. I smoked for 10 years and have small-airways lung disease. Now tell me: Do you think the cigarette companies are being truthful when they say smoking isn't harmful?"

—Patrick Reynolds

Stress

Stress is by far the most misunderstood of all smoking conditions. Ask any smoker and he or she will tell you, with 100% conviction, that they need cigarettes to help relieve all the stress in their lives. The truth of the matter is the very opposite: Smoking is the cause of much stress.

Each of us is equipped with an instinctual defense system designed to help us defend ourselves in times of danger or to cope with challenging situations. From the caveman era it has been called the "fight or flight" response. When confronted by a wild animal the caveman's body defenses were mobilized to either fight the animal or to run away. The hormone adrenaline rushes through the blood and acts as a messenger to all parts of the body. In preparation to be physical, 1200 instant chemical changes take place:

- the heart beats harder and faster (elevating blood pressure)

- there is increased blood flow to the brain (to make one awake and alert)

- secretion of extra acid in the stomach (accelerated digestion for more energy)

- extra blood to the muscles (increased tension)

- more oxygen produced in lungs (rapid breathing)

- increased sweating

When the danger is resolved, all body functions quickly return to normal.

When a smoker lights up, the nicotine acts on the pituitary gland, which raises the blood sugar level and produces a relaxing effect, and on the adrenal glands, releasing adrenaline. Hence the strange combination of simultaneous relaxation and exhilaration.

 Because of the frequent release of adrenaline throughout the day, a smoker's body tends to remain in a state of readiness, ready to do battle. The unused emergency chemicals swirl through the blood and eventually break down into more toxic substances. The physical changes previously mentioned are always present to some degree and stress becomes a constant companion. Energy reserves are drained and bodily systems begin to malfunction. And with it can come irritability, angry outbursts, irrational worries and fears, lack of patience, a reduced ability to rest, poor concentration, memory loss, disturbed and shortened sleep, poor eating habits. Many sufferers report that they are unable to enjoy activities once found pleasurable and that life in general terms seems joyless and uninteresting. This exhaustion stage can lead to long-term illness, including clinical depression. Negative emotions attract other bad emotions, elevating stress even higher.

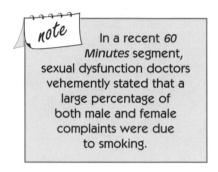

note In a recent *60 Minutes* segment, sexual dysfunction doctors vehemently stated that a large percentage of both male and female complaints were due to smoking.

Sex and stress are not good bed partners. The most common sign that stress is affecting sexual activity is a lack of desire, but may also lead to other physical symptoms as impotence in males and an inability to reach orgasm in females. Smokers experience decreased blood flow to the genitalia, causing erection problems in males and diminished stimulation in females. And because people do not realize that stress is dampening their relationship, they may start looking to extra-marital affairs for an outlet. Of course, these infidelities bring on more stress.

Many scientists believe that the chronic bodily arousal of stress depresses the body's immune system, making one vulnerable to a myriad of illnesses, including cancer, high blood pressure, heart attacks and strokes. It's clear to see why smokers have so many more medical problems and conditions.

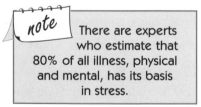

note There are experts who estimate that 80% of all illness, physical and mental, has its basis in stress.

By the way, you may be thinking that there is also good stress. Yes, that's true. We do need a minimal level to feel alert and challenged, but this is normal and undamaging. The occasional jolt from an experience or emotion like excitement can also be good stress, but there are two significant differences:

1) Good stress comes and goes fairly quickly, returning your body to normal, while bad stress tends to hang around for extended periods (the chemicals don't readily get flushed out of the system).

2) Good stress stimulates positive emotions that are benefits rather than detriments.

Stress is finally being understood. This is a subject of study of particular interest for me but I don't want to bog you down with an onslaught of facts and figures. Just know that stress is a terrible, destructive force, and smoking is a major source of stress.

Other medical concerns

> **HINT**))) Half of all smoking deaths strike people in middle age; these victims on average lose 23 years of life. 293,000 brave Americans died in World War II. This year alone, in the U.S., smoking will kill 500,000.

Smoking is the cause of dozens of other problems: everything from back pain to kidney cancer, birth defects and infertility, gum disease, bronchitis, liver cancer, frequent colds and flu, osteoporosis, wrinkling of the skin; the list goes on.

> *It is just such an outrageous infuriating idea that people smoke that It's hard to talk about in rational terms. Everyone has the right to do what they want to their own body, but what I see is all the families who suffer as they watch their loved ones die and are left alone. I can't imagine anything more selfish than smoking cigarettes.*
>
> —Dr. Steven Rosenberg
> Chief of Surgery
> National Cancer Institute

A prominent heart surgeon told me that if everyone stopped smoking today, more than one third of all the hospitals in this country would close in the next 5 years.

—Larry King
USA Today

Good health is the first and most important prerequisite for every other good thing in your life.

—Dr. Ralph Cinque

Wolfman Jack, 55, Jerry Garcia, 55, and John Candy, 43, all died from smoking diseases.

Social pressures

It used to be a person's smoking habits were his or her business. No longer. It has become a big public issue and the public is getting fed up. In California smoking is banned in every public building in the state, even bars. The rest of North America will soon follow. Many singles won't date a smoker, regardless of virtues.

When I smoked I was a "pulsive" person; impulsive, compulsive and repulsive.

—Patty A. Ex-smoker

Today, lighting a cigarette in a restaurant is about as socially acceptable as wandering around spitting into people's salads.

—Dave Barry

Thieves, gamblers and prostitutes nearly all smoke— and so do people in lawful professions, if their behavior requires them to quiet their consciences.

—Leo Tolstoy

Smoking is just a terrible, dirty habit. It was once glamorous,
but now it is a nuisance that no longer interests me.

—Actor Glen Ford

At one time a lot of high achievers were smokers. Only 2% of a recent entering class at Harvard smoked.

More and more employers are refusing to hire smokers because of:

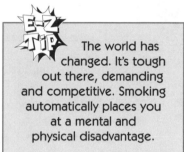

The world has changed. It's tough out there, demanding and competitive. Smoking automatically places you at a mental and physical disadvantage.

- frequent illness

- high stress symptoms

- time loss

- evidence that smoking is counterproductive to work efficiency

But if you think it's tough being a smoker now, take a look at the world during the 17th century:

- ✦ The Shoguns of Japan jailed smokers and confiscated their property.

- ✦ Smokers in Turkey could be beheaded.

- ✦ The Emperor of Hindustan ordered that smokers have their lips slit.

- ✦ In Russia, the Tsar also slit their lips, for a first offense; habitual smokers were put to death.

- ✦ In China, tobacco traffickers were decapitated.

Smoking is a custom loathsome to the eye, hateful to the nose,
harmful to the brain, and dangerous to the lungs.

—King James I
1604

What do you hate or dislike most about being a smoker?

Using a pen or hi-lighter, mark those that particularly apply to you. Add any of your own to the list.

1) financial cost

2) burn holes in clothes, car and furniture

3) late afternoon taste in mouth

4) cigarette "hangover"

5) feeling of being a slave

6) paying more than my fair share of taxes

7) fear of lung cancer

8) criticism and nagging of others

9) being a negative role model, a bad example

10) fear of heart disease

11) pervasive stink of smoking

12) bad breath

13) dental and gum problems

14) looks I get from non-smokers

15) fear of emphysema

16) stained teeth and fingers

17) being trapped in non-smoking places and situations (dinner parties, airplanes, sporting events)

18) frequent colds

19) smoker's cough and phlegm

20) shortness of breath

21) lowered self-respect and self-esteem

22) being a fire hazard

23) feeling weak willed

24) excess skin wrinkling

25) always feeling nervous and jumpy

26) nausea

27) giving my money to greedy cigarette companies

28) knowing I'm a drug addict

29) being part of a disliked minority

31) thought of constantly poisoning my body

32) knowing my health is suffering

33) feeling like a loser

34) thoughts of being dumb and foolish

35) knowing there are thousands of unwanted chemical compounds circulating through my body

36) feeling embarrassed

37) feeling like a criminal

38) feeling like a sucker

39) being irresponsible

40) the pain of needing a cigarette and not having one available

41) the hassle of buying and carrying cigarettes

42) being ashamed to be a smoker

43) smoking in secret

44) feeling persecuted

45) being an outcast

46) always having to say "I'm sorry"

47) being a sexual turn-off

48) feeling of self-contempt

49) plagued by self-recrimination

50) worry about health risk to others

51) feeling helpless

52) feeling angry

53) feeling of being hooked

54) feeling trapped and afraid

55) straining relationships due to smoking

56) feeling frustrated

57) feeling out of control

Yours:

1)

2)

3)

4)

5)

Even if I did smoke, I wouldn't do it in front of anybody, because I wouldn't want them to know how stupid I was.
—Dick Gregory

What's most important to you about being a non-smoker

1) feeling clean inside and out

2) experiencing the surge of pride that comes with a job well done and even more importantly

3) the pride of my loved ones

4) tremendous elation of being free—forever

5) knowing that nothing as ridiculous as a cigarette will ever control my life again

6) every day my breathing will grow stronger and deeper

7) my priceless heart can finally rest and return to a normal work schedule

8) feeling like a capable person, able to get things done

9) so nice to enjoy travel and social situations, not being harassed by a nicotine urge

10) waking up after a sound night's sleep, alert and raring to go

11) saving the cigarette money in a jar for a dream vacation

12) picturing my lungs as they'll be in about two years, pink and healthy

13) losing that irritating, chronic cough, and along with it, the horrible yellow-green phlegm

14) it's great being admired and envied by co-workers and friends

15) the sense of accomplishment is a real boost to my ego

16) easily winning one of the most important battles of my life

17) talking to others without the concern of offending them with my bad breath

18) be on the other side, pitying the poor souls who are still trapped in the jaws of addiction

19) the calm, peace and serenity that comes with being one's own master

20) feeling like a winner

21) fully appreciating the taste and aromas of my favorite foods

22) replacing sluggishness with a newfound vigor and stamina

23) feeling the stress draining away from my body and mind, and with it nervousness, anger and impatience

24) looking and feeling younger and healthier, with a rosy glow replacing the pallor

25) enjoying sex with a new zeal—awakening old desires

26) approaching life with a new confidence, willing and able to tackle new goals and challenges

27) knowing I have freed my immune system to protect me and keep me healthy

28) the knowledge that I may now live an additional 5 or 10 or 20 years, years to enjoy all that life has to offer

29) an appreciation of having every aspect of my life gaining in quality and value

30) a sense of being reborn, given a second chance, of burying the mistake in the past

Yours:

1)

2)

3)

4)

5)

STOP!   IF YOU HAVEN'T COMPLETED THESE EXERCISES, PLEASE DO
THEM NOW! WE ARE IN THE PROCESS OF RE-PROGRAMMING
YOUR BRAIN—FORGING NEW PATHWAYS.

Seeing and believing

Chapter 4

Seeing and believing

Opinions, beliefs and convictions

Truth is beautiful, without doubt; but so are lies.

—Ralph Waldo Emerson

Truth is incontrovertible. Malice may attack it, ignorance may deride it. But in the end, there it is.

—Winston Churchill

Has intelligent life from outer space ever visited Earth? You might answer by saying "I'm not sure, but I think it's likely we are not alone in the universe." This is your *opinion*. Or you might respond with "There must be other life out there more advanced than ours. There's little doubt that at some time in past centuries, we have been visited and investigated." This is your *belief.* Or, "There is physical evidence and numerous eyewitness accounts. I am positive that aliens have landed on Earth many times." This is your *conviction*.

DEFINITION An *opinion* is loosely held and the person is somewhat open to being influenced one way or the other, while a conviction is a rock, able to withstand extreme pressure. A wrong opinion does little damage but an erroneous conviction in certain areas can be devastating.

Back in my drinking days I was totally convinced that life without alcohol was not worth living. And there's no doubt in my mind that, after finishing my jail sentence, I would have gone straight back to the bottle, and further disaster. But fate intervened in the form of my sister, Jan. Before my trial, if I would promise to attend Alcoholics Anonymous meetings, she offered to finance a $5,000 fee for a sharp lawyer who could substantially reduce my sentence. I reluctantly agreed and forced myself, strictly to keep my promise, to attend some meetings. But even through my indifference and disdain, the AA message eventually took hold and the granite of my conviction was eventually ground to dust.

DEFINITION A *belief* is a feeling of certainty about what something means, but it doesn't have the solidity of a conviction. It is backed by trust and some degree of confidence, but the door is not locked to new information or arguments. Beliefs can come from

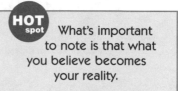
HOT spot What's important to note is that what you believe becomes your reality.

anywhere: TV, your childhood, your parents, past experience, books, advertising, movies, the opinions of others, or even your imagination. They can be right or wrong, good or bad, true or untrue.

If you think you can do a thing, or think you can't do a thing, you are right.

—Henry Ford

Beliefs are a shortcut, a guiding force to lead us away from pain and into pleasure. But often we don't consciously decide what we're going to believe. For whatever reason, once a belief is formed in the subconscious, we accept it as reality and seldom question it. There it remains, until something or somebody comes along with acceptable, contradictory information.

For thousands of years the earth was believed to be flat. In the 1940's smoking was seen to be innocent and, many thought, healthy. Do you remember first hearing the cruel truth about Santa Claus, the Tooth Fairy and the Easter Bunny?

Smoking is a manufactured, false pleasure that only limits the quality and quantity of life.

Now let's add some "cruel truth" to your beliefs:

Smoking helps me cope with all the stress in my life.

I hope I've convinced you in the previous step that smoking is the source of much of your stress. The frequent secretion of adrenaline can lead to a constant state of readiness for an "emergency" that never happens. This can at times be seen as your "normal" state. Many smokers don't realize how stressed they were until sometime after they quit.

Life without cigarettes is empty.

Life can feel empty when you don't smoke but still have a craving for cigarettes. When you've completed these steps your desire will diminish to the point that you won't ever want to smoke again, and life will be anything but empty. Look around you, at the people you admire, those that are vital, active, dynamic. Those with lives you envy. Do they smoke? Are they missing out on something? Of course not!

Towards the end of my liaison with cocaine, I suffered through constant nausea, a bleeding nose, terrible anus pain, financial ruin, paranoia and depression, but still, I couldn't imagine a worthwhile life without this grasping drug. Insane thinking? Yes, I believe that all our addictions, including cigarettes, create some degree of temporary insanity. There's a protective mechanism that will go to any lengths to shield its safety and survival. Looking back I can see how bizarre and asinine my thinking had been.

Addictions have a knack of building up their own self importance. They somehow make us believe that they are indispensable cogs on our wheels of life. But what are they really? They are sand in the machinery—sand that will inevitably disable and ruin the machine.

> *Cigarettes benefit from that almost perverse quality in human nature that makes what is despised by some people absolutely irresistible to others.*
>
> —Gordon Dillow

I don't much care about reaching old age.

Live fast, die young and have a good-looking corpse! For years his son and his doctors urged Yul Brynner (the dynamic hero of *The King And I*) to quit smoking. His smiling comeback was always "I don't want to live to be an old man."

He got his wish. Shortly after he turned 60, lung cancer struck. Yul fought back with a tremendous act of will but the next four years were a nightmare of pain and humiliation. He could hardly breathe. Sleep was all but impossible and when he did sleep, the medication produced fearful hallucinations. As the cancer spread to his spine, he said to his son, "I couldn't even have imagined this pain."

Being wheeled to the radiation room, the ravaged Yul turned his skeletal face to his doctor of 36 years, "Why the hell didn't I listen to you?"

He filmed a TV spot to be broadcast after his death "Now that I'm gone I tell you. Don't smoke. Whatever you do, just don't smoke."

The man who gave Yul Brynner's eulogy, Alan Jay Lerner, died from smoking. The man who gave Alan Jay Lerner's eulogy, Leonard Bernstein, also died from smoking.

While he was in the hospital dying of lung cancer, Yul called his friend Leonard Bernstein nearly every day. "For God's sake, Lenny," he would say to the famous conductor, "Quit! Look what it's done to me." But Bernstein kept smoking until the day he died of lung cancer.

Most people would rather die than think; in fact, they do so.
—Bertrand Russell

The moment you stop smoking, healing begins. The body, given the chance to use them, has amazing regenerative powers. Take away the poison and you give your body that chance.

With robust health and a winning attitude, the later years can be a treasure; a wealth of experience, financial security, travel, time to read and enjoy hobbies, an "empty nest" with occasional visits from the grandchildren, peace, serenity, freedom. Talk to well-adjusted, vital seniors and most of them will tell you their retirement years are the most precious and enjoyable of all. They also relate that each stage of life has its own unique rewards and gifts.

I've been smoking too long. I'm too old to quit. The damage is done.

The moment smoke touches the lips, it begins to attack living tissue and continues to do so wherever it goes: mouth, tongue, throat, esophagus, air passages, lungs, stomach, and its breakdown products eventually reach the bladder, pancreas, and kidneys.

The happiest ex-smokers I've seen are the ones who were hooked the longest. Regardless of how many years you were trapped, rejoice in the fact that you escaped without a major disease. Consider yourself fortunate and be thankful for an opportunity to return your body and mind to a state of health.

> **HINT** You're going to be pleasantly surprised at how much better you think, act and concentrate when the interference of cigarettes and craving is gone.

I'm one of the lucky ones; I smoked for 40 years and got away with it. At 50, my blood pressure was dangerously high and I couldn't climb a flight of stairs without gasping. Today at 55, the doctor has told me I have the heart rate of a man in his 20s. My lungs are clear and healthy and the rest of my body is working beautifully. I feel I could run a marathon.

I can't work or concentrate without cigarettes.

Because less oxygen is available, a smoker's brain simply can't function as well. With a puff or two the concentration level seems to increase, but it's the very temporary alertness triggered by the jolt of adrenaline. It's hard to think and concentrate when

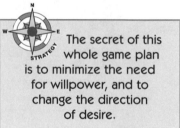

> **STRATEGY** The secret of this whole game plan is to minimize the need for willpower, and to change the direction of desire.

you crave a smoke. As well, there can be a strong connection (association) between your work and smoking. You've always done the two together. Smoking becomes a part of working.

I've long been an avid poker player. And cigarettes once were part of the game. Chips, cash, cards and cigarettes, each a necessary component. About ten years ago I had quit smoking, painfully, for almost a year. During that period, I played only a total of 20 minutes of poker. I simply could not concentrate, could not get comfortable, and could not enjoy the game. Sitting at the table became an ordeal.

Once I devised and used my system of quitting successfully, I was playing cards the very same day, also successfully.

I'm just too weak. I've tried everything and nothing works.

When the desire and craving to smoke is high, the willpower needed to quit is high, and predictably the failure rate is high. But we have a plan and strategy to drastically lower the craving to smoke (and greatly increase the desire to not smoke).

Using willpower alone is so difficult, so discouraging, and so defeating, it's no wonder we feel so weak. To make the entire process easier, much easier, just have faith. When the day for your last cigarette comes, your mind will be in a different place, the right place. Continue to keep an open mind.

I'm physically active, eat well and watch my weight.

Cigarettes won't hurt me. Cigarettes exact a price. Somewhere along the way, regardless of how healthy you think you are, it will be time to pay. The price will be suffering or premature death, and likely both. "For every action there's a reaction," Cigarettes always come with consequences. This is a fate you can't tempt and get away unscathed. One way or another, when you play, you pay.

Everything in life involves some risk.

There are smart risks, calculated risks and dumb risks. Where would you place smoking? If you choose really stupid behavior, you will experience severe negative repercussions. If you choose to live recklessly and without regard for personal safety, a likely consequence is pain and suffering.

I think many people attach excitement and glamour to gambling, to risk. The same attitude that keeps casinos rich can be applied to smoking. I honestly remember feeling "special" for having the guts and chutzpah to defy the numbers, to buck the odds. I truly was a man, strong and brave and daring.

The difference between genius and stupidity is that genius has its limits.

If they were as bad as they say, they'd be illegal.

Nothing is illegal if 100 businessmen decide to do it.

—Andrew Young

They are legal because:

- The Tobacco Institute is the richest and most powerful lobbying organization in the land, spreading distortions, propaganda, and misinformation.

- The government reaps enormous taxes from cigarette sales, and gains valuable foreign trade revenue to reduce the burgeoning deficit. *Money makes the rules. And who has more money than the cigarette companies?*

In a "60 Minutes" interview, a Bear Stearns financial analyst called cigarettes a poison disguised as a consumer product. The next day he was fired.

The support of politicians and political parties by those associated with tobacco interests is unconscionable. How can Americans believe political promises for health care reform when both parties seem to be associated with an industry that disseminates disease, disability and death.

—C. Everett Koop
Former Surgeon General

You have to be ready to quit. I don't think I'm ready.

I'll quit:

- when my life is less hectic

- when I lose x number of pounds

- when the price goes past___$

- when I turn __

- on my next vacation; and on and on and on and. . . .

> *note* Experts say that low-tar cigarettes are even more dangerous to your general health than the regular strength.

You have to be ready! This is likely the #1 belief of all smokers. For most, "ready" never comes. I say you make your own "ready," by being *willing* to keep an open mind towards worthwhile, honest and sincere information. There are seeds of discontent in your mind, the beginning of a search for freedom. Give your desire to change a chance to grow. Don't fight it. Be *willing* to change.

> *You are never ready until you begin.*
>
> —Rudolph Dreikus

> *Delay is the deadliest form of denial.*
>
> —C. Northcote Parkinson

I'm minimizing the health risk by only smoking low-tar cigarettes.

If this were only true. A smoker develops a level of nicotine need that remains pretty much constant. When I switched to "light" cigarettes, I smoked more, took larger drags, inhaled deeper, and usually covered the air holes with my lips. For years I was very proud of myself for making this sacrifice for my health.

An added problem is that the flavorants used to make low-tar cigarettes taste palatable produce more and higher levels of toxic chemicals.

Cigarettes have been my best friend.

And what friends they were. When I was feeling low, there they were to pick me up. They understood my frustration and anger and were there to calm me. In good times and bad they never left my side. We worked together, partied, drank, laughed, cried, traveled. Friends I could count on, through thick and thin.

When finally I fully opened my eyes I came to see this "friend" as a living thing, a demon that had invaded my mind and body. It was always the boss. It would say "I want what I want when I want it, and I WANT IT NOW!" If I didn't jump, I'd suffer. This thing is not only a brute, it's crafty. It tricked me. It made me believe we were meant for each other, that we needed each other. It gave me illusions of pleasure, relaxation, independence, and control.

The truth is this ogre robbed me. It stole my money, my time, my self-respect and my freedom. It sapped my will, drained my health and, given the chance, would have left me for dead.

 If cigarettes were people they would be the lowest form of humanity. They lie, cheat, deceive, steal, spread disease and suffering, and kill without remorse. If they were people, society would clear them off the streets. If they were people, society wouldn't give them the luxury of being locked up for life—every last one would be executed.

If you have beliefs different from those above, list them here:

1)

2)

3)

4)

5)

Of each, ask these questions:

- Where did I learn this belief? Was it a reliable, plausible and honest source?

- How is this belief wrong, or exaggerated, or irrational, or perhaps even absurd?

- What price will I have to pay if I continue to hold on to this belief?

- Is this belief preventing me from getting what I really want?

With what you've learned thus far about cigarettes, smoking and yourself, compose a few new empowering beliefs that will guide you in the right direction: (for example: Stress is my nemesis, and smoking generates stress. With health, my golden years will be filled with excitement, fun, comfort and love. Cigarettes are not my best friend, but my worst enemy. My body is a temple that must be protected against trespassers.)

1)

2)

3)

Here's two additional beliefs that will really drive you:

1) **I MUST** quit smoking. Too often change doesn't feel like a "must." It's something we should do or would like to do someday. There's no urgency. As you progress through these steps, add up the reasons as to why you must change. Keep asking yourself, "If I continue smoking, what pain will be waiting in the future? If I quit, what pleasures can I expect? How will I feel about myself? How will this affect my family and friends?"

2) **I CAN** quit smoking. You will soon realize that you have all the resources you need; the power of your mind, a step by step plan, and a new understanding. If

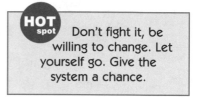

HOT spot Don't fight it, be willing to change. Let yourself go. Give the system a chance.

you don't yet have it, faith in yourself is just around the corner.

If you think you are beaten, you are. If you think you dare not, you don't. If you'd like to win, but think you can't, it's almost a cinch you won't. Life's battles don't always go to the stronger or faster man; but soon or late the man who wins is the one who thinks he can.

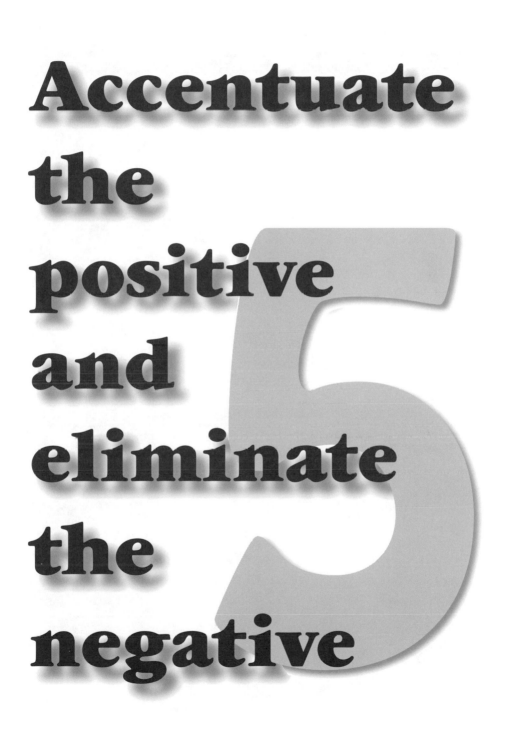

Accentuate
the
positive
and
eliminate
the
negative

Chapter 5

Accentuate the positive and eliminate the negative

A mountain of words have been written on the subject. It is the basis of entire philosophies. Napoleon Hill, the father of personal achievement, placed it on the very top of his list of greatest riches. *A positive mental attitude*. But what is it really? I used to think that positive thinking was a way of fooling yourself. After all, how could you *not* think negatively? Reality, most of the time, is simply not positive. As usual, I was a little bit right, but mostly wrong.

Positive vs. negative

DEFINITION

A *positive mental attitude* is a collection of mental habit patterns, a behavior program in the subconscious,that guides and directs thoughts and actions in a direction that helps you rather than hurts you, that builds rather than destroys. It leads to good decisions rather than bad.

Like all mental programs, it is shaped by a combination of related habits of thinking and acting. It is a consistent positive way of reacting and responding to various situations. Here's an example: In New York City, as the light turns to "Walk," a man steps off the curb and is almost hit by a speeding taxi. He shakes his fist, curses the driver, and angrily stomps away. For hours he seethes about the"idiot" that almost ran him down. He's in an agitated state for the rest of the day, snapping at people,grinding his teeth, and getting little accomplished. In the same situation, another man jumps back from the taxi and thinks, "Wow, that was close! At this minute I could be bleeding on the street, or even dead. This is my lucky day. The driver was careless but it must be tough trying to make a living as a taxi driver in this city. I'm going to treat myself to a special lunch. It's great to be alive!" The remainder of this person's day is happy and productive.

DEFINITION

A *negative mental attitude* focuses on the problem. It leads to disempowering emotions like worry, fear, anger, frustration and doubt. And where does that take us? To procrastination and inactivity. We feel terrible and don't do anything to alleviate the problem.

A positive mental attitude focuses on solutions and goals. It activates empowering emotions like faith, courage, initiative, perseverance, hope, and confidence. Action takes over. We feel great and get things done.

Let's face it, when you really come down to it, despite our best efforts to avoid them, life is a long series of problems. The happiest and most successful people are those that can solve any problem, big or small, that comes their way. In the workplace you get paid according to the size of the problem you can fix. A kid working the counter at McDonalds solves a small problem of getting the Big Mac from the warmer to the customer. He's paid minimum wage or thereabouts. The CEO of General Motors has the problem of coordinating a billion dollar operation to show an acceptable return to stockholders. If he is successful, what do you guess he gets paid?

The power of the positive

Who are the achievers of our society? Who are the happy ones? Who wins the special man or woman? Who makes the most money? Who most *enjoys* their money? Who has a zest and passion for life? Yes, the problem solvers. And who are the best problem solvers? The positive people.

Positive thinkers recognize each other and tend to stick together. They belong to an informal club. But do you want some good news? The club is wide open to anybody that discovers the "secret." There's plenty of room for all that qualify. Every new member is welcomed with open arms because he or she, by virtue of their attitude, adds value to the world and all those around them.

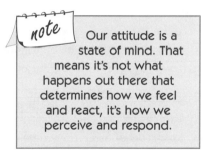

note Our attitude is a state of mind. That means it's not what happens out there that determines how we feel and react, it's how we perceive and respond.

What a planet this would be if, somehow, every individual had the knowledge, incentive and training to win a positive mental attitude. Nothing that can be acquired is more valuable.

We are always in charge of our actions. And we act and think according to the master program in our brains. Think the worst and you'll get the worst. Think failure and that's what you'll get. Think positive and you'll be led to success.

Enemies of the state

The fiercest enemy of a positive state is fear, and where does fear come from? It's not from the possibility (or even likelihood) of losing your job or your spouse or your money or your health. It's how you choose to see a situation. You manufacture fear in your head; so in effect you are capable of being your own worst enemy. Allowing fear to dominate your mind leads to focusing on the problem, which then leads to a rash of unwanted results. Here's a definitive definition from Napoleon Hill: "Fear paralyzes the faculty of reason, destroys the faculty of imagination, kills off self-reliance, undermines enthusiasm, discourages initiative, leads to uncertainty of purpose, encourages procrastination, makes self-control an impossibility, takes the charm from one's personality, destroys the possibility of accurate thinking, diverts concentration of

E-Z TIP Solving problems develops faith and self-confidence.

effort, masters persistence, turns willpower into nothingness, destroys ambition, beclouds the memory, invites failure in every conceivable form, kills love, assassinates the finer emotions of the heart, discourages friendship, invites disaster in a hundred forms, leads to sleeplessness, misery and unhappiness." *Whew!*

Faith and fear cannot occupy the same space. You fight fear by always attacking, always looking for solutions. Never, never dwell on problems. You may not always be able to control what enters your mind, but you are in charge of what remains there.

> *Do the thing you fear and the death of fear is certain.*
> —Emerson

Building your positive attitude

If a good attitude is so important and valuable, why doesn't everybody have one? Unfortunately, much of our attitude is shaped, without our really being consciously aware of it, by the environment. A good part of this programming (remember, if we don't take charge of our own programming, the subconscious will develop its own) is formed in the early stages of our lives and altogether too much of it is negative. Childhood is filled with "don't, can't, bad, stop," and so on. A result of destructive criticism and frequent punishment is stress-related pessimism, a fear of failure, a tendency to play it safe. As we grow up, we are exposed to legions of negative people, wars, violence, tragedy, brutal competition, ridicule, hatred, and self-doubt. We couldn't even count on formal education to light the way. Schools didn't teach us about goal setting, self-esteem, or building confidence. Consequently, many of us grew up with a strong, and sometimes dominant, negative mental attitude.

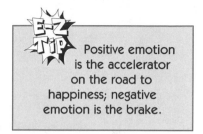

Positive emotion is the accelerator on the road to happiness; negative emotion is the brake.

But, really, what is the ultimate purpose of life? Is it to have a million dollars, a successful career, to sail around the world, to help humanity, or to raise a wonderful family? It may be any or all of those things, but what we're all really after is one thing—*happiness*. That is the supreme goal. And you know what? The long-term level of happiness in your life is directly related to the level of your positive mental attitude. They go hand in hand, cheek to cheek, arm in arm. If you consistently have either one, it's almost a guarantee you have the other.

We all know or have heard of workaholic tycoons that never smile, movie stars who wallow in drugs and self pity, million dollar athletes that never have a good word to say about anything. Even power, fame and money, sometimes, do little to ease a troubled, negative mind.

Everything in my life, every little happening, problem, disruption, worry, or result seemed so-o-o-o important, until I recognized that I am just a tiny speck on a minuscule ball of matter in the incomprehensibly vast continuum of space, and for the briefest flicker of time. Consider this: there are 100 billion galaxies in the Universe. Each galaxy has 100 billion stars. The nearest star after our sun is 25 trillion miles away.

Here are some of the keys to your happiness, to building a master "positive mental attitude" program:

Your behavior is a result of the state you're in.

Understand that anger, confusion, anxiety, fear, sadness, depression and frustration leave you paralyzed and powerless. Determine what's causing this emotion and act immediately to find a remedy. If it's a condition that can't be fixed, get it out of your mind. If you don't take conscious control of your mind, you lay yourself open to be at the mercy of whatever is happening around you.

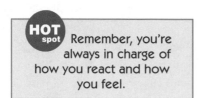

HOT spot Remember, you're always in charge of how you react and how you feel.

This, of course, is easier said than done. But understand that these emotional states fall into patterns of thinking and the road to positive thinking takes new and better routes. Whatever it takes, begin to build better patterns; do something, do anything, take action, find a solution, make a change, make a decision, walk away. Do whatever necessary to break the old pattern. Don't get stuck in the problem. *You're in charge*. If you just look for it, there is always a solution!

The easiest way to change any state is to change your focus.

Your mind can only hold one thought, good or bad, at a time. Simply direct your thoughts in a direction that helps you and makes you feel good. Let's say you have just taken a $1,000 beating in the stock market. Dwelling on the loss ("Why was I so greedy? I should never have listened to that idiot. The things I could have done with that money. How could I have been so stupid?") can only make you miserable and helpless. Change your focus. Realize that this is only a small

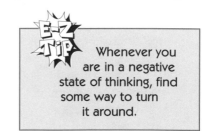

E-Z TIP Whenever you are in a negative state of thinking, find some way to turn it around.

speed bump on the road of life. What's more important than what you've lost? Your career, your health, a loving family, your honesty and integrity? Money can always be made. Realize that this won't be particularly important a year from now. Vow to learn what it takes to make better investing decisions.

When I quit smoking I learned the power of focus. In previous attempts, I would always look, with envy and longing, at a person smoking. When they inhaled, I inhaled. They were lucky, being able to smoke. I felt so sorry for myself. Then I learned to use focus to my advantage. As they inhaled, I saw their black lungs, their palpitating hearts, the poison flowing through their veins. I was so lucky to be free, to be clean, to be healthy. I felt such pity for those still locked in their self-made prisons.

Focus can be directed with questions. Ask yourself, "Is this line of thinking hurting me, or making me feel bad, or stopping me from taking action? What could I think about to make me feel good, to give me the incentive to make changes?"

Whenever he thought about it, he felt terrible. And so, at last, he came to a fateful decision: he decided not to think about it.

Know the power of questions.

Thinking is nothing more than asking and answering questions. Without realizing it we are constantly asking ourselves questions like "What does that mean? What should I do now? Is that really true?"

But we also ask, "Why does this always happen to me? Why can't I ever do anything right?" A negative *why* question is dangerous because your brain will find answers like, *Because you're stupid. Because you're lazy. Because you don't follow through.* Why questions make you feel scared, inadequate, unlucky and impotent.

 Whenever adversity strikes, rather than asking a *why* question, ask *what* or *how* questions, "What can I learn from this? How can I use this? What's good about this? (Looking back at your life, didn't some disaster in the past eventually turn out to be valuable in some way?)

Disaster struck when I entered the world of crime. Financially and emotionally desperate, I attempted to rob a small, suburban bank. At 10 a.m. on the day before New Year's Eve, I threw back a double shot of cheap rye whiskey, never guessing this would be the last time liquor ever touched my lips. Two hours later, with the four employees laying face down on the floor, there I was, holding a real-looking pellet gun, trembling and fidgeting, waiting for the time lock vault door to open. (Yes, I really was that stupid and befuddled, standing there for the longest 10 minutes you can imagine.) Spotting the police car through the window, I made a run for the getaway car, and as I opened the door, BOOM. I was thrown onto the console and within seconds handcuffed to the door. The bullet had shattered the main artery in my right arm, spraying the dashboard and windshield with blood. My life of crime was over, almost before it began.

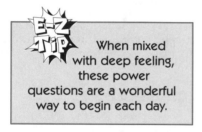

When mixed with deep feeling, these power questions are a wonderful way to begin each day.

Sounds like a horrible experience, doesn't it? Well, as it turns out, this was the best thing that could have ever happened. It might have been the only way I would have ever gone to an A.A. meeting. Jail gave me time to dry out, to think, to escape all the outside pressure, to build a little faith and hope. It was exactly what I needed at the time. The direction of my life had changed. Although there were a host of trials and tribulations still to come, I was heading up rather than down.

Of course, I didn't have the wherewithal to know that then, but if something seemingly bad would happen now, I would immediately start asking questions, "What's good about this? How can I use this experience to help me in the future? What can I learn from this? How important will this be a year from now?"

Your subconscious holds reams of information and ideas, just waiting to be released. For example if you want to lose some weight, ask questions like How would I look if I lost x pounds? How would it make me feel? How can I reach my goal comfortably? What can I do to lose weight and enjoy the process? *Questions are the answer.*

Tony Robbins has come up with a great set of morning questions:

1) What am I happy about in my life right now? (Or, what could I be happy about if I wanted to be happy?)

2) What am I excited about?

3) What makes me proud?

4) What am I grateful for?

5) What's most enjoyable about my life?

6) What am I committed to?

7) Who do I love and who loves me?

Always the beautiful answer who asks a more beautiful question.

—E. E. Cummings

Contrast

My preferred method self-torture was once comparing my dismal, uneventful, third class life to the likes of Tom Cruise, Dan Marino and Donald Trump. This would absolutely verify the bitter truth of my inferiority in every department—looks, brains, talent, ability and ambition. If I felt bad before, this exercise took me lower than a snake's belly. "What's the use of trying? I'm nowhere now and I'm going nowhere better."

Often I didn't have to look as far as Hollywood, Miami or New York. In my own backyard there was always someone around with the car I had always wanted to own, the woman of my dreams, the ambition I always lacked, the winning, witty personality, the looks of a Greek statue, the gold-plated confidence, the pockets full of money—things I would never have, things an inferior person like me had no right to deserve.

I'd wallow in a bog of self-pity and depression for a few days, smoking, drinking or doing drugs, filling my face with sweets, anything to try to ease some of the pain, anything to suspend the truth. And it worked—for a while. Then, inevitably, there it was again, staring me in the face, the last thing I wanted to see, the thing I feared and loathed—reality.

Boy, have I changed! I discovered that the real world is where all the pleasures and rewards are. I can now use contrast to my advantage: to steer me away from pain, to fuel my enthusiasm, to get me excited and thankful. Every day I count my blessings, beginning with the reading of a list titled, "I'm so lucky because:

- I was born and raised in a wonderful, free, prosperous country like Canada.

- My organs all work, my brain survived the onslaught, and I have the use of all my limbs.

- I no longer need or want a glass of Scotch, a line of cocaine, a toke of grass, or a cigarette.

- I have people to love that love me.

- Every night I have a comfortable bed to sleep in, and every day I have a choice of the best foods that the world has to offer.

- I've killed the assailants of fear, stress and depression. I sleep the sleep of babes.

- My children are happy, and make me content and proud.

. . . and so on. My list is up to 22 items and growing. *Truly, don't all of us have so much to be thankful for?*

If at some time during the day my state of mind needs a boost, I turn to hyperbole. This is my thinking process:

- I'm not doing life, like John Gotti, in a maximum security prison.

- I'm not suffering in a hospital bed with the terminal stages of lung cancer, hairless, frail, with radiation burns on my body, nauseous, pain oozing from every pore.

- I'm not lying in a flea-bitten hotel or some filthy alley, broke, and dying for a drink or a fix.

- I'm not walking the streets of a third world country, starving, and having no idea where my next meal was coming from.

- I'm not standing in a line on a Moscow street, hoping, when my turn comes, that the bread hasn't run out.

- I never have been, and probably never will be, tortured.

Contrast is such an easy and fun way to make yourself feel great. Try it for a few weeks and, like me, you will soon have a new habit pattern that will automatically direct your thinking to a good place. You may never suffer through self-pity again.

Now, it's your turn.

"I am so thankful and grateful for:

a)

b)

c)

d)

e)

f)

g)

h)

i)

j)

k)

l)

m)

o)

p)

Pretending

If we feel a particular way, we tend to act that way. But if we don't feel excited or positive, we can simply pretend that we are and in a couple of minutes actually start feeling excited and positive. For example: if you are sluggish first thing in the morning, get out of bed and pretend this is the brightest day of your life; stand tall, throw your shoulders back, clap your hands hard and repeat with enthusiasm, "I feel terrific! I feel terrific!" Believe it or not, in a short time you will actually start feeling pretty good.

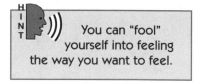
HINT You can "fool" yourself into feeling the way you want to feel.

If you're having trouble getting into this book, pretend that it is the most fascinating, interesting book you have ever read and, within five minutes, you will begin to enjoy the material.

Physiology

When people don't like how they feel, they: eat, smoke, sleep, drink alcohol, or do drugs. (Think—Elvis Presley, Marilyn Monroe, John Belushi.) Or they can use positive strategies like walking, exercising, singing, or making love. When people are depressed their heads hang down, shoulders are stooped, mouth is down-turned and breathing is shallow. An "up" and happy person stands tall, shoulders square, smiling and breathing full.

To instantly feel good, repeat the procedure from the preceding section; simply stand straight, clap your hands together hard a few times, put a big grin on your face and shout, "I feel great." It really works. Try it right now. C'mon, don't take my word for it. *Stand up right now and prove it to yourself.*

Affirmations are an effective way to influence the subconscious

DEFINITION

An *affirmation* is a statement that is personal (*I*, not *we*), positive ("I will, I am," rather than "I won't," or "I'm not"), and in the present tense, the *now* (the subconscious cannot deal with the future, such as "I will be . . .").

When going through the quitting procedure, I still had a few lingering doubts and reservations. It was time for an affirmation. I chose: "I am a grateful and happy ex-smoker." First of all I drew up a list of all the reasons there were to be thankful and happy. Then, six or seven times a day, once always at the beginning and end of each day, I would read the list, and repeat the affirmation five times, with as much body tension and enthusiasm as I could muster, out loud in front of a mirror, or driving down the road, or with thought alone in some public place. Remember that emotion is what really drives this message deep into the inner mind. Well, within 2 to 4 weeks, when this pattern was accepted by the subconscious, my thoughts and actions changed and *I actually became a grateful and happy non-smoker.*

Most people just can't accept that something this simple can really work. But take my word for it—I've used affirmations to help eliminate stress, depression, fear and other problems. It took me many years to make a decision to try the first one—I sure am thankful I did.

Visualization

Visualization is another skill that took me years to accept and use. Because our brains are so visually oriented, it's the most powerful mind-influencing technique known. There are images that remain in the mind for decades. I can picture my first grade classroom, the lake where I learned to swim, my first bike, Sputnik circling the earth.

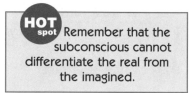

HOT spot Remember that the subconscious cannot differentiate the real from the imagined.

It's not essential that the picture be clear. You can visualize with feeling, emotion, and even vague impressions. The impact and clarity improve with practice. The more you think about it, the more clear and precise it becomes. Realize that you visualize all the time; pictures are always a part of your thinking. Take a minute or two now to cover your eyes and re-live the best vacation of your life. Where did you stay? Who were you with? What was the highlight of the trip? How did you feel when you left? That wasn't so hard, was it? Can you imagine yourself landing on the moon, the weight and bulk of the spacesuit, kicking up the fine moon dust, jumping six feet off the ground?

To use this method, close your eyes (even better, cover with a mask or dark cloth) and picture yourself in a situation where you already reached your goal. For example, see yourself as a successful, happy ex-smoker up on a stage receiving an award for your accomplishment. In the first row of the audience are your kids, your wife,

E-Z TIP Of all stimuli, images have the greatest impact on the subconscious. The more you can think in pictures, the quicker you become that person in the picture.

co-workers, your best friend, and that one person who thought you would never do it. Everyone is standing and clapping. Your eyes grow moist. You've never felt so strong, proud and grateful.

Or, another scenario where, on the one year anniversary of your quitting, a party is given with you as guest of honor. All the important people in your life come up to hug, kiss, and congratulate. Emotions of love and pride flood your body. During your day, play this scene often on the screen of your mind. Your subconscious, once it has accepted this picture, will give you the appropriate thoughts and actions of that successful, happy person.

A few years ago, I had to produce a speaking video within a month. I had been practicing with a camera for many weeks, but just could not get over the fear. As soon as the "on" button was lit, my anxiety shot up and every take was a fiasco. Time was running out, and in desperation I tried visualization. Half a dozen times a day, I covered my eyes and saw myself completing a successful video, ending with my thanking the cameraman. (I also used an affirmation, "The camera is my friend, my partner, my power!") You know what? When the actual day arrived, I walked into the studio with *no anxiety*. I was truly comfortable, calm and competent. The video was no Hollywood production, but it worked well, served the purpose, and I have had absolutely no camera fear since.

But, be warned. When you think negatively, or worry, you produce vivid mental pictures of the situation you fear. Your body becomes aroused just as if the situation you imagine is actually happening. Adrenaline is released and the physical anxiety symptoms follow.

Whatever you do, don't underestimate the enormous potential of affirmation—and particularly visualization—to help make you the person you want to be. And, it's fun! You get to create all sorts of interesting and enjoyable situations. *This is a preview of life's coming attractions.*

Negative emotions lead to regrets.

Negative emotions like anger, resentment, envy, and guilt seem to pop up in our minds far too often, and they make us say and do things we usually regret. One powerful way to rid yourself of these destructive feelings is to practice *forgiveness*. One of the major causes of mental illness is an inability or unwillingness to let go of grudges or anger towards yourself or people you feel have hurt you.

The first people you have to forgive are your parents, even if they have passed away. Regardless of all the pain you went through as a kid, every missed present, spankings, fights, poverty, cruelty, and injustice—simply

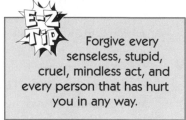

Forgive every senseless, stupid, cruel, mindless act, and every person that has hurt you in any way.

make a judgment that they did the best with what they had, and you forgive them for everything. It's really as easy as that. Just do it and it's over, forever. You'll never have to go through the turmoil again. Realize that it's unimportant as to who was right or wrong. It doesn't matter. You're not really doing this for them; it's to free you. This is a relic of the past, but many adults take this emotional distress to their graves. What a terrible price to pay for something that can't be changed.

Now, forgive *everyone else*. Always keep in mind, you're doing this for yourself, not them. They likely don't care or remember. Your resentment in effect actually gives a person power over you without his even knowing.

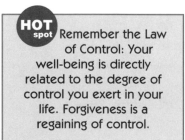

Remember the Law of Control: Your well-being is directly related to the degree of control you exert in your life. Forgiveness is a regaining of control.

This approach may seem too simplistic to you. After all, how can you just immediately forgive a grudge that has been a part of you for years? I'll say it over again; it's easy, just do it. Let the words flow out of your mouth,

"I unconditionally and forever, forgive _____

for_____ ."

Most importantly, you have to forgive yourself for every dumb, selfish, embarrassing, hurtful, and inane thing you've ever said or done. Life offers an unlimited supply of opportunities to make a fool or an ass of one's self. Everybody makes mistakes, lots of them. But, regrets serve no purpose but to keep them alive in your mind. If possible, make amends to anyone you have hurt. Most people are very willing to accept an apology, but if not, remember you are doing this for yourself.

Forgiveness frees the mind and the soul from an awful burden. The burden and strain of guilt, resentment and anger. Forgiveness is like discarding bricks from a knapsack on a long trek. Suddenly you are standing taller, walking faster, smiling, and free. The world looks brighter and more inviting.

Like water off a duck's back

I used to let everything get to me. A traffic jam when I was late for dinner, watching someone bite their nails, a person in front of me with 11 items in an express grocery checkout, a stain on my tan jeans, missing the trailers at a movie—there seemed to always be a reason to be upset or angry.

Then I changed my philosophy and my way of thinking. It was time for a new habit pattern. Using the techniques in this section, I simply made up my mind to let nothing bother me. For example, caught in a

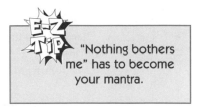

"Nothing bothers me" has to become your mantra.

long line at a bank, I would think *Nothing bothers me. Nothing bothers me.* Aren't we fortunate to have this dependable, safe, government controlled banking system? I feel sorry for the people in this line that are all stressed out. Five or ten minutes really isn't going to affect my day. I can use this time to count my blessings, to plan my day, to strike up a conversation." My life has improved immeasurably since adopting this attitude. Looking for the good in every circumstance, I always find it.

May you be granted the serenity to accept the things you cannot change, the courage to change the things you can, and the wisdom to know the difference.

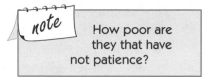

note

How poor are they that have not patience?

Don't take life so seriously!

Get your priorities straight. Worry not at all and smile always. Life is an adventure. Life is a gift. We're not meant to struggle; we're here to learn, to enjoy, to grow, to have fun. A little effort and practice can make spectacular changes in your appreciation of life. Never forget, a positive, healthy mind is the greatest of all treasures.

Napoleon Hill's 12 Riches of Life

1) a positive mental attitude

2) sound physical health

3) harmony in human relations

4) freedom from all forms of fear

5) the hope for future achievement

6) the capacity for faith

7) a willingness to share one's blessings

8) a labor of love as an occupation

9)   an open mind on all subjects

10) self-discipline in all circumstances

11) the capacity to understand others

12) financial security

I'd love to see Christ come back to crush the spirit of hate and make men put down their guns. I'd also like just one more hit single.

—Tiny Tim
Tiptoe Through the Tulips

As a confirmed melancholic, I can testify that the best and maybe the only antidote for melancholia is action. However, like most melancholics, I also suffer from sloth.

—Edward Abbey

Burning
the bridges

Chapter 6
Burning the bridges

It is in your moments of decision that your destiny is shaped.
—Anthony Robbins

Take a trip through time

Take a deep breath. I want you to honestly and realistically think about the price you are paying to satisfy your craving to smoke. What has it cost you in the past and what is it costing you now? What are you losing in terms of self-esteem, money, health, pride, freedom, confidence, and self-respect? Stop and really concentrate on each of these. I want you to suffer the pain, the disgust, the sense of loss. How do you feel about yourself? What do you think is happening inside your body? What sort of a role model are you for the special people around you? Think of the tremendous price you're paying, physically, emotionally, financially, spiritually, and socially.

Carry yourself five years into the future with the weight of all these costs. Bring along all the accumulated baggage of anger, frustration, physical pain, self-loathing, and disappointment. Feel yourself dragging this burden for five more years. Look in the mirror. Living with all this weight on your shoulders, how does your face look? Healthy and glowing, or sad and gray? Are you smiling or frowning? How do you feel about yourself, having lived another five years with this demanding ogre on your back? What's been the cost? *Don't just think it, feel it!* Experience the pain.

Now drag yourself ten years into the future. Feel the tremendous weight of all that guilt. After another 100,000 cigarettes, what must your lungs look like? Do you feel heavy and weak and old and tired? What can you say to that person in the mirror? What can you say to your loved ones? How much are you willing to pay for this fallacious, two-faced, counterfeit pleasure?

Snap back to the present, today, the now. Stand up, take a couple of deep breaths, clap your hands and shake off the oppression of that negative state. Again, place yourself five years in the future, but this time having been cigarette-free for all that time. Do you feel energized, alive, and enthusiastic? Do you have a sense of being free, and in control? Have you found your life has changed far more than you would have ever expected? How is every day better? What have you gained? Do you work better, play more, attempt challenges, eat better, and enjoy more activities? Has your self-esteem and confidence grown? Do you feel calm and collected? Is your stress level down? Do you like and admire that person in the mirror? Do you now see that quitting smoking is the best thing you could have ever done for yourself? Are you proud of yourself for having the guts and good sense to have made this fateful decision?

> *Life rewards action. The world couldn't care less about thoughts without actions. People don't care about your intentions; they care about what you do. "The road to hell is paved with good intentions." The natural tendency is to make excuses, and in a society of procrastinators, it's the norm.*
>
> —Philip McGraw

Being a highly effective person

Stephen Covey describes these traits in highly effective people:

- they have an ability to create in their minds a picture of the future

- they have a deep inner awareness of right and wrong—a conscience

- they feel responsible for their own lives

- they take the initiative to make good things happen

- they have an ability to keep commitments and promises

- they are able to admit a mistake and learn from it

- they have a willingness to learn from others

- they have an ability to act

- they can make the right decision quickly

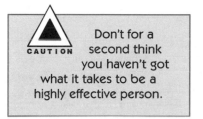

Don't for a second think you haven't got what it takes to be a highly effective person.

I'm an effective person, but please don't think I'm special or different in some way. I'm just an ordinary guy who, after a lifetime of failure, finally learned how to use my "greatest asset" to get the things I want. It's a well-worn statement, but in my case, particularly true: "If I can do it, anyone can do it."

Do the thing and you will have the power.

—Emerson

You have everything you need, in that three pounds of gray matter between your ears. All you have to learn is how to get it working for you, and that's what this step system is all about. Don't you already feel more capable, and more confident? Is your level of faith rising? Can you sense success waiting for you just around the next bend or two?

> *It is surprising to what extent men come to regard their habits*
> *as necessities: How habit enslaves the body and mind; how it*
> *perverts the judgment and subsidizes the reason.*
>
> —Henry Gibbons M.D.

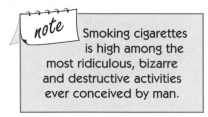

note Smoking cigarettes is high among the most ridiculous, bizarre and destructive activities ever conceived by man.

When I was finally able to be completely honest with myself, I discovered that smoking is truly a filthy, disgusting, and dirty habit. If that's not enough, it is also in a class by itself—a vicious, cunning and deadly addiction. The world of the future will look back on this time and shake its head with amazement and disbelief.

Really, really think it through! You pay thousands of dollars a year to inhale burning noxious toxins and poisons into your body, clogging your lungs with molasses-like tar, ruining your entire cardio-vascular system, immobilizing the immune defenses, and raising stress. You lay yourself wide open to the worst of illnesses and diseases, to anger, guilt, slavery, and a cornucopia of antagonistic emotions. (Take a minute to run over the lists in Step 2.) What a terrible price to pay, to experience a false pleasure, an illusion. *You have become the horse and life has become the rider.*

> *Common sense is not so common.*
>
> —Voltaire

How to make the change

There's a myth in our society that says change takes a long time, that the cost will be high, the struggle mind-bending. This is simply not true. Change can come quickly, comfortably and permanently.

You stand at the spot where endings and beginnings meet, handcuffed by the past, but now about to be free. I want you to make that decision now, to pick your *quit day,* 10 to 14 days from now, and vow to rid yourself of cigarettes forever. No ifs, ands, buts, or maybes. You'll be done on that day. All you have to do is have trust in me, this step system, and the power of your brain. This is a partnership that will work.

I pledge to banish cigarettes from my life forever,

at _____ A.M.\P.M. _____(day) _____(month)____(year)

signed _____

witnessed _____

There, good for you! You've done it! Start feeling proud of yourself right now, because you deserve it. Don't you feel a great sense of relief? The bridge is burning brightly. In the future, you'll always see this as one of the great decisions of your life. Some year down the road, you'll be lying on a beach in a tropical paradise, sipping a delicious cooler, and remembering this auspicious day. In the meantime, take my word for it; in a couple of weeks, *you won't smoke, you won't want to smoke, and you'll never smoke again.*

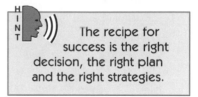

The recipe for success is the right decision, the right plan and the right strategies.

This is a good time for you to once again visualize the person you want to be. *Don't go any further* until you've taken five or more minutes in a quiet, private area, with a covering over your eyes, to see and feel yourself as an enthusiastic, elated, and admirable ex-smoker. Make it an exultant and exciting script with you the center of attention and the star of the production. Every positive emotion you can muster adds power to the image being impressed on your subconscious. Replay this scene for a couple of minutes, at least four or five times a day, for the next two weeks. Before you know it, suddenly, you will have truly and magically become that person.

The "smoking highway"

7

Chapter 7
The "smoking highway"

<h3>What you'll find in this chapter:</h3>

⮕ The driving forces behind human nature

⮕ Our greatest need and fears

⮕ Keeping a record of your smoking habit

⮕ Discovering your "triggers"

⮕ Getting ready to quit

The secret of success is learning how to use pain and pleasure, instead of having pain and pleasure use you. If you do that, you're in control of your life. If you don't, life controls you.
—Anthony Robbins

There is a driving force behind all human behavior. Whether you realize it or not, everything you do is for one of two reasons. *Everything you do is for a need to avoid pain or a desire to gain pleasure.* You will usually do more to avoid pain than to gain pleasure. Either consciously or subconsciously, every decision you have ever made in your entire life is controlled by one or both of these forces. Pain and pleasure drive the decisions as to your work, what you wear, how you think, your relationships, where you live, how you look, and your habits. Even something like procrastination. Why is it you don't do something when you know you should? It's likely you attach more pain to taking action than putting it off.

The pain/pleasure principle

Your subconscious is wired to guide your decision making, and to keep you out of pain and into pleasure. Unfortunately it is susceptible to making false associations by not being capable of interpreting or judging your patterns of behavior. In seeking to protect and reward you, your subconscious makes errors in what to approach and what to avoid.

Smoking is a perfect example of just how this process works. The pleasure I gained from first trying cigarettes was:

- breaking the rules

- stepping into the adult world

- being accepted by my friends

- being a rebel

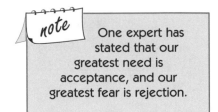

One expert has stated that our greatest need is acceptance, and our greatest fear is rejection.

With cigarettes I could avoid the pain of:

- being seen as a chicken

- rejection by my friends

Going on, as I grew older and continued to smoke, the reasons changed, but clear and strong patterns of gaining pleasure and avoiding pain were firmly entrenched in the subconscious. My brain was simply giving me the behavior, thoughts and actions needed to satisfy the desires and cravings that smoking created.

Most of us decide what to do based on what's going to cause pain or pleasure in the short term, rather than the long term. Immediate gratification is more important.

Very often it's not the actual pain that drives us, but the fear that something will lead to pain. It's not reality, but our perception of reality. I wouldn't attempt to ask a girl out because the potential for rejection and embarrassment conjured frightful pain.

The reason people continue to smoke is that they link so much pain to quitting, and more pain to losing their pleasure. So the answer seems obvious, doesn't it? All we have to do is smother the entire act of smoking with a heavy blanket of pain, while whipping open the dark drapes to reveal the array of pleasures awaiting the ex-smoker. We create a world so attractive, so bright, and so appealing, that resistance ceases to be an option.

Your path to the "super highway"

Your "craving to smoke" program, this pathway in the brain, is like traveling down a private super highway. It's fast and smooth and wide and comfortable. Dozens of times a week, without much thought or planning, you cruise down the road, just enjoying the uninterrupted ride. Well, we want to change all that. Everything we can do until your quit day to disrupt, weaken or scramble any or all of the patterns that make up your "smoking" program will add a crack to the road, a bump, or a detour. We want the ride to be rough, slow, uncomfortable and irritating. The more damage we can do to this highway, the lower the level of pleasure. When you get tired of avoiding or navigating all the fissures and roadblocks, your brain will look for an alternate, friendlier route.

The new route is being built. Every waking hour of every day, positive thoughts and actions add a little more surface to the new road. By your quit day, the old "smoking" highway is ravaged, and the "smokeless" autobahn is ready for high speed traffic. The choice will be undeniable.

DAY 1: For the first day all you have to do is keep a record of each cigarette and the circumstances in which you smoked. The location is your home, car, office, outdoors. What were you doing—shaving, talking on the phone, drinking coffee, walking, watching TV, etc? Was there any particular purpose to having this cigarette—to relax, to get stimulated, to relieve boredom, to socialize, etc.?

TIME	LOCATION	ACTIVITY	PURPOSE IF ANY

DAY 2: Were you perhaps surprised by the number of cigarettes you used (studies have shown that most smokers, unknowingly, underestimate the daily number they smoke by about a third), and by how many served no particular purpose?

DEFINITION

A *trigger* is a person, place or event that provokes you to automatically reach for a cigarette. It's a switch that flashes "Time to smoke!" Here are some of the common triggers and associations that may affect you:

- talking on the telephone

- watching TV

- driving

- drinking coffee

- a work break

- alcohol

- after a meal

- after sex

- playing card or other games

- reading a newspaper or book

- leaving your place of work

- during a walk

List those in your daily routine (plus any unique to weekends):

1)

2)

3)

4)

5)

6)

7)

8)

9)

10)

Reroute your patterns

Let's start scrambling these patterns in your brain by disrupting the routine and by mixing some pain in with your pleasure.

Until your "quit day"

Throw as much confusion into your smoking patterns as possible. For each of your trigger/associations make at least one change. If you're an avid coffee drinker, switch to fruit juices or herbal tea. Hold the telephone with your opposite hand. Stand instead of sitting. Cut out alcohol. When watching TV sit in a different chair. Use coffee breaks to take a walk or to read. Avoid your usual smoking companions. Keep your cigarettes in another room or in some awkward location. Change brands. Hold your cigarette in the opposite hand. Do *anything and everything* you can to take your brain out of its comfort zone. (Remember these changes are only necessary for a few weeks, not the rest of your life.)

Delay having every cigarette for at least 5 minutes

It's much easier than you think, and before you light up, read some of the items on the lists from Step 2, what you most dislike or hate about smoking and/or what you would most enjoy about being a non-smoker. Just before you flick your *Bic*, think with feeling and concentration about one particularly important point on that list.

As you're smoking, try to keep your mind in a negative state

Focus on the 4,000 chemical compounds in every drag, the pain of being an addict, the black coating in your lungs, rich tobacco companies, the nicotine hitting your adrenal glands—*anything that will lessen the pleasure and increase the pain*.

In a large clear glass jar, save a quantity of butts and ashes and keep it in a place where you spend a lot of time. Use this as a frequent reminder of what you are about to leave. As well, these butts will be needed for an exercise in the final step.

DAY 3: Re-read Step 1. Pick one or two affirmations from this list or make up your own. For each, think hard and deep as to why this statement does or should apply to you. Then, repeat each affirmation, with emotion and enthusiasm, five times, five or six times a day.

- I'm worth it.

- Every day I am getting better and better.

- I'm a grateful ex-smoker.

- I'm a happy non-smoker.

- I love my life.

- I am strong, I am invincible, I am human.

- I only think positive.

- I have faith in myself.

- I feel terrific.

- I like myself.

- I am powerful.

- It's easy to change.

Yours:

1)

2)

3)

 DAY 4: List 2 or 3 smoking situations that caused you some well-remembered embarrassment.

Here are three from my past:

• Driving down the highway, my girlfriend and I were in the midst of a heated battle. Thinking the window was open I angrily flicked my butt and got sprayed with a shower of sparks and ash. The car careened and I just managed to reach the shoulder without crashing.

• In the early days of non-smoking flights, I was on my way to England. But 13 hours without a cigarette was out of the question. Surely a smart guy like me could find a way. In the washroom I hung my head deep in the toilet bowl, lit up and flushed simultaneously. In seconds the smoke detector shrieked and there was a pounding on the door. Two hundred sets of eyes followed me back to my seat. The next 12 hours seemed like 12 days.

• Many years ago, in a moment never to be forgotten, a girl I knew saw me pick up a butt from the street.

Yours:

1)

2)

3)

DAY 5: Re-read Step 2. Pick the one most compelling reason for your desire and need to quit smoking. It might be to see a grandchild graduate or get married, to take a vacation of a lifetime, to be fully in control of your life, to make someone important very proud, to compete in a triathlon, or to retire in Fiji. This is a goal that will drive you, lift your spirits, and get your blood flowing. Write it down and read it with feeling at least 3 or 4 times a day. Really focus on the words. Give it your complete attention every time. Concentrate. Create a mental picture that becomes stronger and clearer each day.

I must and will quit smoking because _____

_____

_____

_____

_____

DAY 6: So often we tend to focus on failures and shortcomings, rather than successes. What accomplishments and achievements, as far back as childhood, stand out in your mind? Did you conquer a fear or phobia, win a race, receive an academic award, get a date with someone special, learn a skill, or break a bad habit?

1)

2)

3)

4)

5)

DAY 7: Re-read Step 3. Procrastination was once my "silent killer". I never did today what could be possibly be put off till tomorrow. This became a "deadly" mental habit pattern that murdered my ambition, self-esteem and reputation. Behind the door to procrastination, I always found an ample supply of booze, drugs and self-pity.

> *Never do tomorrow what you can put off until the day after tomorrow.*
>
> —Mark Twain

To change, I had to face the terrible price I have paid and will pay if it continues. I now, usually, avoid that pain plus have the ongoing pleasure that comes with getting things done well and on time. I simply replaced

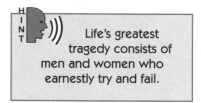

Life's greatest tragedy consists of men and women who earnestly try and fail.

one habit with another. It's really not that hard. Like Nike says, "Just do it."

You can more easily *avoid* failure by realizing and understanding the *reasons* behind failure. Napoleon Hill compiled this list. Rather than just reading these points, spend a little time on each one. Think! Be honest with yourself. So often just a little effort is all that is needed to break out of some old, silly, useless, or destructive pattern of thinking.

1) Not having a well-defined goal that is written out and visualized.

2) Lack of ambition to aim above mediocrity. Indifference to paying the price required for the good things.

3) Unwilling to exercise discipline to take charge of their lives.

4) Unfavorable environmental influences during childhood by family and peers.

5) Procrastination. Time is never right to make a committed decision.

6) Lack of persistence. Giving up at first sign of defeat.

7) Negative personality.

8) Uncontrollable desire for "something for nothing"; a magic bullet.

9) Lack of committed decision.

10) Allowing fear to rule their minds.

11) Over-caution. Everything must be exactly right.

12) Superstition.

13) Lack of concentration of effort. Failure to make goal a priority.

14) Lack of enthusiasm.

15) Dishonesty.

16) Egotism.

17) Guessing instead of accurate thinking.

DAY 8: Re-read Step 4. Here's a relaxation technique to help reduce stress and anxiety:

Either lie down or sit up straight in a chair with your arms hanging free. Clear your mind and concentrate only on what you're doing. Close your eyes and take five long, deep breaths—your body automatically relaxes with the higher concentration of oxygen. Now, start by tensing only the muscles of your feet and calves. Count to five and relax. Take one very deep breath. Next, tense your thighs. Count to five and relax. Another deep breath. Repeat this procedure with your buttocks, abdomen, arms, clench your fists, shoulders, neck and face. Now remain still. If you feel tension anywhere, tense that muscle to five and relax. Trying not to think about anything else, take another couple of deep breaths expanding the abdomen rather than chest, and let yourself go limp for a minute or two.

For the next week or two, relaxation will be a valuable ally. Don't allow yourself to get uptight. Take the time to relax as often as need be. But don't expect to become a good relaxer immediately.

Like any new skill, you have to practice and work through the initial discomfort. If necessary, force yourself to take the time and effort to complete this routine a half dozen times. By then you'll understand and appreciate the results.

DAY 9: Re-read all of Steps 2 and 5. These are valuable weapons in the last confrontation.

This is the time you want to decide whether to use Zyban or any of the nicotine replacement aids. I personally have mixed feelings, but don't want to discourage you from a tool that can be helpful. If you have really bonded with the concepts and ideas in this book, if your confidence level is high, you should be comfortable without any outside help. If you need a little added support, make use of it. The product that seems to offer definite aid is nicotine gum.

For the remaining days until your Quit Day, attempt to saturate your brain with a flow of unrelenting, beneficial thoughts. Every time a pleasurable notion about smoking or a fearful one about quitting comes to mind, replace it immediately with one that helps. Be on the lookout constantly for ways to disrupt or break the old patterns.

Fill your subconscious with words and pictures of the person you want to be. Every action or thought used in building the new desire to quit program weakens the old craving to smoke. Anything that damages the old helps the new. Quantity is the key. Repeat! Repeat! Repeat! *Repetition is the mother of skill.*

> *Within 20 minutes after you quit smoking, blood pressure, pulse rate and body temperature return to normal; within 24 hours, risk of sudden death from heart attack decreases, and within 48 hours, nerve endings in the mouth and nose begin to regenerate.*

Q-day: Storming the beaches

Chapter 8

Q-day: Storming the beaches

Geronimo! The closing battle is about to be fought and it's time to start firing! You have the weapons. You've trained, sweated, and drilled, and it's time to vanquish the enemy. You've seen the cigarette for what it really is: a sinister, sneaky, malicious, avaricious, repugnant, vile, and venal bully. You don't want this demon anywhere near your world.

The end is near

Now it's time for the final cigarette, and we want this to be a memorable but not a pleasurable experience. You may balk at what I'm about to propose but I hope you'll understand the value. It may appear to be juvenile or silly, but this act will leave an electrifying and lasting impression in your subconscious. An indelible impression!

Here's what to do: Take a last cigarette and destroy the remainder of the pack. No, don't give them away; don't leave them on the kitchen table; don't hide them—"just in case"—*demolish them!* Tear each one into little pieces and flush them down the toilet. Bring your jar of old butts to the bathroom. On a large plate, dump one or two cups of butts and ashes, and pour in a half cup of water. Stir it into a lumpy, thick paste. In front of a mirror, grind your face in the mix until you have a grotesque "smoker's mask." Light the last cigarette while facing the mirror. Watch the dirty smoke curling through your mouth and nose. Think cancer, chemicals, slavery, filth, phlegm, and everything you hate and fear about smoking. Be grateful and thankful that the end has come.

But, don't expect this ogre to quickly throw down its arms and surrender. Be prepared. It will scream, scuffle, brawl, and claw. This is a street fighter with no scruples, morals or sense of fair play. It will attack and defend with fingernails, a kick, a garbage can lid or a broken bottle.

But if you know what to expect, you can duck, slip, feint and counter attack. Here's what's coming at you:

- emotional confusion and depression

- anxiety and irritability, anger for no apparent reason

- restlessness, teeth clenching, trouble sleeping

- diarrhea or constipation, flatulence

- sense of grief or mourning

- wide mood swings, hostility, defensiveness

- feeling of abandonment, betrayal, of being isolated. Resentment and remorse

- feeling of hopelessness and helplessness

- hunger, particularly for sweets

- dry mouth, coughing, aching joints

- queasiness, sweats, lightheadedness, headaches

Looks like a menacing lineup, but you have more than enough weapons to overpower and outsmart this devil, once and for all. In about three days its main energy source, nicotine, will be all but depleted and all of its powers will waggle, waver and wane.

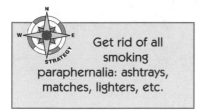

Get rid of all smoking paraphernalia: ashtrays, matches, lighters, etc.

During the battle, every hour is a victory. Every hour the ogre weakens. Feel the tremendous power you hold. The war is all but over and you're about to fully occupy enemy territory—and to the victor go the spoils. Rewards will flow continuously for the rest of your life!

How to keep the peace

Declare your car, office and home smoke-free zones. If others don't like it, that's their problem. Be selfish of your space. Do what you can to remove the smell and memory of smoke; clean your clothes, sheets and drapes, air the car, scrub the ashtrays. *Remember* it is at home that we are most vulnerable, at our weakest, quick to give the enemy a "second chance."

It's particularly important during this time to keep your mind focused on good thoughts. Step up the affirming, visualization, reading lists and whatever else you think might keep you on the right track. Keep your mind clear of all damaging and destructive intruders. Defend the fortress of your mind.

The main battle is over, but there are still pockets of resistance here and there, often well camouflaged. Be intensely aware (and beware) of these areas and situations that can activate the urge to smoke. When you run across one, see it as a huge, bright, fluorescent red *danger sign*. Either get yourself away, change your focus, or concentrate on some type of resolution or solution. Use whatever weapon or tactic it takes to subdue the threat. Fight! Don't let circumstances control you. *Often, the best defense is a strong offense.*

- Any social gathering, particularly with alcohol, that raises your anxiety level. (Alcohol raises the blood sugar level very quickly, signaling the brain with the need for a cigarette.)

- Conflicts, a fight or argument with a family member or co-worker.

- Any sort of emotional upset like depression, anger, irritation or sadness.

- Feeling lonely.

- Having to cope with pressure, like a work deadline, or end of the month bills.

- Taking a coffee or lunch break from work.

- Having something to celebrate, a promotion or birthday or a killing in the stock market.

- One of the most dangerous things you can do is watch, with envy, a person smoking. This is where you must direct your thinking, force yourself to feel pity for that person, to see all the terrible consequences to come, to calculate the price they will eventually pay for this egocentric indulgence.

- Remembering that a cigarette was once the reward for finishing something, a day's work, a chore or assignment, some distasteful duty.

Tips and tactics

Chapter 9
Tips and tactics

Here are eleven tips and strategies to smooth the way:

1) *Be sure that whatever it takes to conquer cigarettes remains your #1 priority.* Don't let anything or anyone stand in the way of this goal. If ever there is a time in life to be selfish, this is it.

2) *Be extra good to yourself.* Make a list of small hourly or daily rewards: a movie, banana, sunflower seeds, sugarless gum, music break, a few minutes to lie on the grass, a break to daydream, lunch at your favorite restaurant, or a phone call to a friend. Promise yourself some bigger rewards in the future, a weekend getaway next month, or a new car next year. You're worth it!

Daily Rewards	Future Rewards
a)	
b)	
c)	
d)	
e)	
f)	
g)	
h)	
i)	
j)	

3) *Keep yourself out of pressure situations.* Where possible avoid situations that offer temptation. Don't worry about what people say or think. They likely just don't understand. It sounds cruel, but if they're not allies in your campaign, they are enemies. Ask yourself, "Will they help me, or hurt me?"

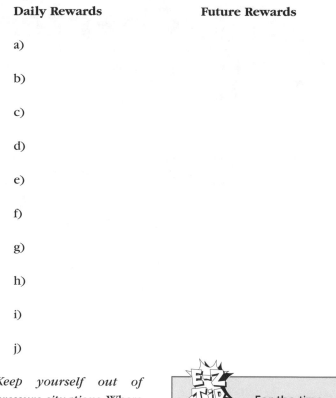

For the time being, stay clear of groups that smoke. Why make it hard on yourself?

4) *Let everyone know that you've quit smoking.* Then you'll have the pleasure of their seeing that you actually did it.

5) *Never forget why you quit smoking.* Continue filling your subconscious with the many advantages of being a non-smoker. Read your lists, over and over and over. It may be inconvenient and perhaps tedious, but every good thought adds another strand to the new pathway. When the highway is complete, you'll know it. The job will be done and you'll be tooling down the 'smokeless' freeway with carefree abandon.

6) *Discover the wonderful world of pleasure and fitness of walking.* As well as gaining the benefits of physical exercise, you can work on solutions to problems, listen to music or motivational tapes, 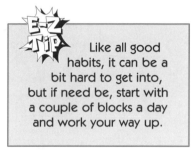 enjoy the beauty of nature, bond with friends or family, or simply appreciate a little quiet time in a raucous world. A thirty minute to an hour's walk every evening will add so much to your life:

   • your mind will work better,

   • you'll feel a sense of calm, serenity and happiness

   • you will feel more alive and alert

   • you'll sleep better and wake up refreshed. My 80-year-old mother walks at least three miles a day and is the happiest person I know.

7) *Avoid coffee and alcohol*, but drink lots of water and fruit juice.

8) *Take time to breathe deep, to stretch and relax.* This lowers the heart rate and stress level. Plus, it just plain feels good.

E-Z TIP Like all good habits, it can be a bit hard to get into, but if need be, start with a couple of blocks a day and work your way up.

9) *Find exercises or games to keep your mind and hands busy.* When is the last time you enjoyed working on a crossword puzzle? Or, how about starting on a new hobby?

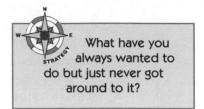

What have you always wanted to do but just never got around to it?

10) *Congratulate yourself often.* You should be so proud of carrying through all that has to be done. You deserve success.

11) *Use all this newfound information, attitude and confidence to help someone else to quit smoking.*

Weights and measures

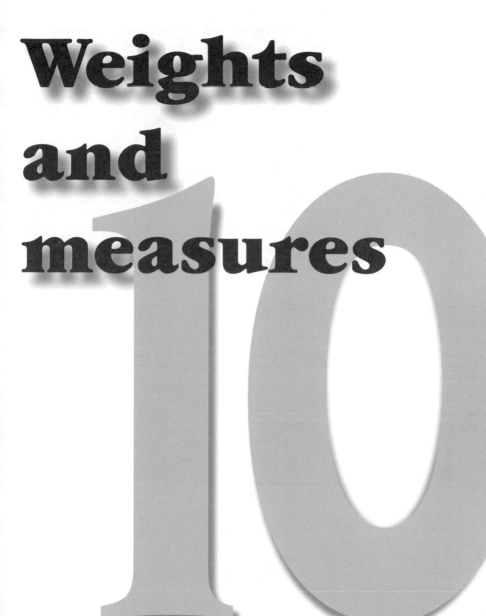

10

Chapter 10

Weights and measures

Smoking and weight loss

note

Yes, smoking can keep your weight down, but it does it in ways that are just so harmful. Our bodies are resilient, but simply cannot cope with constant, long-term punishment. Smokers are often thin (and unhealthy) for these reasons:

1) The normal functions of digestion and metabolism are in chaos because of the unrelenting, perpetual injection of adrenaline into the system. The body is prepared for a fight that never comes.

2) They often substitute a cigarette for a meal. *Food is not a luxury!* Wholesome food is the energy and fuel needed to keep us running, to heal our ills, to fight viruses and infections, and to keep our brains humming.

3) Nausea can kill the appetite. It's hard to think about food when your stomach is churning.

4) Chemical toxins in smoke blunt the senses of taste and smell. Eating is a diminished pleasure.

This present-day obsession with thinness has had a terrible influence on people, particularly girls and women. Many females would rather "die" than be fat. Smoking is such an easy, and convenient method for keeping the pounds off. But it's like choosing to always walk down sinister alleys in the dead of night. Sooner or later you're going to get mugged and beaten, and maybe killed by a gang of "consequences." It's not a question of if, but when.

What to be careful of

Many ex-smokers return to a healthier state with a weight gain of 5 to 7 pounds, but here's a few of the potential problems that may arise:

Blood sugar

A smoker gets regular jolts of blood-glucose when nicotine hits the pituitary gland. Until your body adapts to the change you will have a craving for sweets. When blood sugar drops, hunger pangs set in, either for a cigarette or a snack, and the first impulse is to reach for a chocolate bar. Fight this urge with sugarless gum, fresh fruit, dried fruit (you may be surprised at how good it is), or sugarless mints.

Simple carbohydrates like: candy bars, cake, white bread, pasta and ice cream enter the bloodstream too fast. Blood sugar rises quickly, but the food is quickly absorbed and blood sugar then takes a fast drop. A half hour later you are hungry again.

Foods rich in protein and complex carbohydrates provide the body with a steady stream of glucose, which keeps blood sugar and appetite steady and under control. They also provide nutrients to keep you alert and fiber to decrease the appetite. Generally these foods are poultry, fish, meat, vegetables, fruits, whole grain breads and dairy products. Take care to minimize the use of high fat foods like marbled meat, whole milk or cream, and most cheeses.

The food substitute

A new ex-smoker often feels a need to substitute the lack of cigarettes with food. The need is triggered by the feeling of "empty hands." The answer is to keep as busy as possible: walk, doodle, bowl, listen to music, take pictures, garden, wash the car, read a book, or call friends. If you do snack, use the list above and add pretzels, raw vegetables and whatever lo-cal, lo-fat foods you can find. This may not sound too appetizing, but you'll soon develop new tastes, new habit patterns, and a comfort zone that will add, rather than subtract, to your long-term health and happiness. Just give it a chance. Scaling the "wall of discomfort" takes a little time and patience, but there are acres of rewards on the other side.

Make up a list of "busy" activities:

1)

2)

3)

4)

5)

6)

7)

8)

9)

10)

A reawakened sense of taste and smell

Foods will take on delicious new tastes and aromas once your senses are free of the effects of smoking. You will be tempted to indulge in bigger portions and extra helpings. Be careful. Always leave the table a little hungry. Be willing to learn new and better habits. I've come to love fruit and vegetables, and I feel 20 years younger.

This is the perfect time and chance for you to learn about the things that can add so much to life. Your body is a marvelous creation—a Rolls Royce. Many people treat this gift like clunker transportation, to get them through life with a minimal amount of cost and maintenance. Shower your Rolls Royce with the respect and care it so richly deserves.

Release traps

This demon of addiction is like a zombie from a "B" movie. Long after, what we think is its death and burial, it rises, waiting for a tiny crack, any opening, to invade once again. It's a grinning specter that loves conflict and crisis, a moment of weakness, a time that's you're not paying attention. It strains its ears to hear beckoning words like these:

- "I'll never get this work done. What does he think I am, a robot?"

- "Honey, we just won $5,000 in the lottery!"

- "Thank God I'm finished. What a relief."

- "I don't know how I'm going to make that payment this month."

- "I've been so good. It's my birthday."

- "I've almost forgotten what it tastes like. Just one puff for old time's sake."

- "You want me to hold this cigarette for you?"

- "How could she have died so young. What am I going to do without her?"

- "If she says one more word, I'm going to scream!"

- "I feel so empty. Something is missing."

- "This is wonderful Scotch. Just one cigarette to be social."

- "I'm so grouchy without cigarettes. I don't think I was ready."

- "I'll have a cigar but I won't inhale."

- "He's left me. What does it matter."

- "I'm going to just have one cigarette to prove that I'm the boss."

For one brief instant defenses are down; reason, rationality, will and commitment are suspended or forgotten. The ogre has its opening. Opportunity knocks. This is a time of testing, the moment of truth. Who will win?

A slip is a painful experience. The person has a drop in self-esteem and a feeling of helplessness. The worst of negative emotions are released; self-doubt, depression and guilt. *A slip is the demon's doorway.*

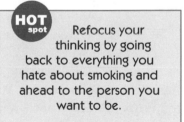

HOT spot Refocus your thinking by going back to everything you hate about smoking and ahead to the person you want to be.

You must have prepared and ready an arsenal of combating weapons. Command yourself:

- "Stop! Don't do it!" Walk away from the danger zone immediately. Give yourself time to think.

- "If I have this cigarette, how will I feel about myself in the morning?"

- "If I have this cigarette, who will I disappoint?"

- "What do I love about being a non-smoker?"

- "What do I hate most about smoking?"

- "One cigarette, or even one puff, is a gamble I cannot afford."

- "I will not allow this obscene ogre back into my life!"

If somehow the slip occurs, treat it as a learning experience and just go on. Don't moan, groan and belabor the fact. Put it behind you immediately. Life, as a whole, is full of slips. The losers succumb and fall by the wayside, battered, bruised and beaten. The winners get up quickly, dust themselves off, put a wry smile on their faces, and with a flash of determination, run back onto the playing field.

> *Many of life's failures are people who did not realize how close they were to success when they gave up.*
>
> —T.A. Edison

 Never, ever forget. **You're in charge** of how you think, what you think! Not it, or them, not anyone or anything. **You are in charge!** Don't you dare give up control of your life. It's your property, your assets, your power. If you have to fight, fight! Protect and defend it at all costs.

Smoke-free
smiling

Chapter 11

Smoke-free smiling

I've come to believe that cigarettes are evil. They enslave our minds, sap our will and poison our bodies. Smoking is a rapacious, reckless act of self-destruction, suicide on the installment plan.

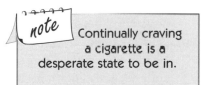

note Continually craving a cigarette is a desperate state to be in.

This is a drug-ridden society. We are the most drugged people in the history of the world. We contaminate ourselves day in and day out and have come to see this drugging as normal.

I'm so gratified and excited that you've stuck with me through all these steps, and now here you are, joined with the ranks of successful and happy ex-smokers. You had the guts and good sense to make a decision, follow a plan and overcome a barrage of enemy artillery. You are a special person and I congratulate you.

To the victor go the spoils

You have now learned the tremendous power of the mind and I'm sure you'll use this triumph over cigarettes as an incentive to make other worthwhile changes in your life. You may never sell yourself short again.

A year after conquering cigarettes, I finally had the courage and conviction to tackle my biggest problem. I was 51 and had endured moderate to deep suicidal depression for at least ten days per month, right back to childhood. I'm alive today for one reason only, a belief that my death would have devastated my mom, dad and sister. We were a family of worriers and each of them would have, in some way, felt personally responsible. Guilt and grief might have covered their world with a perpetual dark and dense cloud. Luckily for all of us, I saw the taking of my own life as the ultimate act of selfishness. I just couldn't leave them with all that potential, probable pain.

In retrospect, overcoming depression without drugs was the most formidable accomplishment of my entire life. I saw it as scaling a snow-capped mountain. Where once I might have been besieged by terror and intimidation, I now had the grit, faith and tools to find a way up. Unexpectedly, I enjoyed much of the climb. There were slips and falls and stumbles, but the exhilaration at the summit made every step worthwhile. I had made it. Tears of pride rolled down my face. I knew in that moment, at last, I was fully in charge of my life. Nothing would ever control me again.

> *Victory over self is of all victories, the greatest and most rewarding.*
>
> —Plato

With victory come the rewards; the gift of accomplishment, the gift of health, the gift of pride, the gift of freedom and the gift of time. Use them well.

"Optimists club" creed

Promise yourself:

- To be so strong that nothing can disturb your peace of mind.

- To talk health, happiness and prosperity to every person you meet.

- To make all your friends feel there is something of value in them.

- To look at the sunny side of everything and make your optimism come true.

- To think only the best, to work only the best, and to expect the best.

- To be as enthusiastic about the success of others as you are about your own.

- To forget about the mistakes of the past and press on to the greater achievements of the future.

- To wear a cheerful countenance at all times and give every living creature you meet a smile.

- To give so much time to the improvement of yourself that you have no time to criticize others.

- To be too large for worry, too noble for anger, too strong for fear, and too happy to permit the presence of trouble.

Daily journal

Day 1:

Day 2:

Day 3:

Day 4:

Day 5:

Day 6:

Day 7:

Day 8:

Day 9:

Day 10:

Day 11:

Day 12:

Whatever you need to know, we've made it E-Z!

Informative text and forms you can fill out on-screen.* From personal to business, legal to leisure—we've made it E-Z!

PERSONAL & FAMILY

For all your family's needs, we have titles that will help keep you organized and guide you through most every aspect of your personal life.

BUSINESS

Whether you're starting from scratch with a home business or you just want to keep your corporate records in shape, we've got the programs for you.

FEDERAL & STATE
Labor Law Posters

The Poster 15 Million Businesses Must Have This Year!

All businesses must display federal labor laws at each location, or risk fines and penalties of up to $7,000!
And changes in September and October of 1997 made all previous Federal Labor Law Posters obsolete;
so make sure you're in compliance—use ours!

State	Item#	State	Item#	State	Item#
Alabama	83801	Louisiana	83818	Ohio	83835
Alaska	83802	Maine	83819	Oklahoma	83836
Arizona	83803	Maryland	83820	Oregon	83837
Arkansas	83804	Massachusetts	83821	Pennsylvania	83838
California	83805	Michigan	83822	Rhode Island	83839
Colorado	83806	Minnesota	83823	South Carolina	83840
Connecticut	83807	Mississippi	83824	South Dakota not available	
Delaware	83808	Missouri	83825	Tennessee	83842
Florida	83809	Montana	83826	Texas	83843
Georgia	83810	Nebraska	83827	Utah	83844
Hawaii	83811	Nevada	83828	Vermont	83845
Idaho	83812	New Hampshire	83829	Virginia	83846
Illinois	83813	New Jersey	83830	Washington	83847
Indiana	83814	New Mexico	83831	Washington, D.C.	83848
Iowa	83815	New York	83832	West Virginia	83849
Kansas	83816	North Carolina	83833	Wisconsin	83850
Kentucky	83817	North Dakota	83834	Wyoming	83851

State Labor Law Compliance Poster
Avoid up to $10,000 in fines by posting the
required State Labor Law Poster available from
Made E-Z Products.

$29.95

Federal Labor Law Poster
This colorful, durable 17³/₄" x 24" poster is in
full federal compliance and includes:

- The NEW Fair Labor Standards Act Effective
  October 1, 1996
  (New Minimum Wage Act)

- The Family & Medical Leave Act of 1993*

- The Occupational Safety and Health
  Protection Act of 1970

- The Equal Opportunity Act

- The Employee Polygraph Protection Act

* Businesses with fewer than 50 employees should display reverse
side of poster, which excludes this act.

$11.99
Stock No. LP001

See the order form in this guide to order yours today!

Index